PRAISE FOR

THE 20-20 CREATIVITY SOLUTION

"John Dillon practices what he preaches. He preaches the importance and accessibility of creativity and he practices it in his guitar making, his radio producing, and his writing—in this instance, writing an excellent hands-on guide to the creative process!"

—ERIC MAISEL, PhD, America's foremost creativity coach and author of *Coaching the Artist Within*

"The simple steps in this book will activate your 'Inner GPS for Success' and guide you home to your untapped Authentic Self—one that is naturally creative and brilliant!"

—STEFANIE HARTMAN, publisher, speaker, and CEO of S.H.E Inc.

"*The 20-20 Creativity Solution* is a refreshing departure from the usual right-brain focus of creativity—it turns out you need both hemispheres to contribute 'intuitive' and 'rational' components to creative endeavors. Moreover, creativity is not limited to a few fortunate individuals but is a human capacity accessible to all of us. With warmth, compassion, and clarity, John Dillon tells the delightful story of how he rediscovered his creativity, and offers an accessible guide to how you can bring creativity into your life."

—REX E. JUNG, PhD, neuroscientist and creativity researcher, Mind Research Network

"John Dillon reminds us that creativity is our essential nature and our authentic expression. His book heralds a return to the natural rhythms and ways of creativity that are our birthright but have been nearly lost in the Industrial and Information Ages. *The 20-20 Creativity Solution* presents easy steps to start our personal and cultural renaissance. A lovely bedside book!"

—Gail Carr Feldman, PhD, author of *From Crisis to Creativity* and *Taking Advantage of Adversity*

"*The 20-20 Creativity Solution* is a well-researched textbook on creativity and a very provocative read, both informative and inspirational. John Dillon deftly transports us on his own life journey, and in the process shows us the universal thread of creativity that runs through us all. We are all uniquely creative, all filled with that creative spark, but many of us don't truly believe it. Reading and working *The 20-20 Creativity Solution* will do much to turn that spark into a creative fire that will light the world."

—Freebo, *Artist's Way* instructor, award-winning singer/ songwriter, and former bassist for Bonnie Raitt, John Mayall, and Ringo Starr

"Creativity is our birthright. Thanks to John Dillon for his essential *20-20 Creativity Solution* that points us in the right direction and offers such useful and effective tools for creative exploration. Brilliant."

—Kristine Maltrud, founder and CEO of ArtSpark, micro-funding and community support for artists

"In *The 20-20 Creativity Solution*, John Dillon captures a special whisper that will awaken an inner spirit that wants to guide you. The exercises give that spirit a voice in a unique and powerful way. It is life-changing!"

—KATHLEEN DESMAISONS, PhD, addiction specialist
and author of *Potatoes Not Prozac*

"John has written a delightful step-by-step guide for anyone seeking a system to develop habits for creativity. The book is easy to read, sincere, earnest, and passionate. A little gem."

—LESLIE KENTON, award-winning writer, TV broadcaster, filmmaker, photographer, and creativity guide

FROM THE FIELD OF BUSINESS
AND LEADERSHIP

"So often in the world of business we fail to tap our creative side in searching for a solution. I have found that creative solutions outside normal bounds are often more readily accepted and cost effective, and easier to implement. John's book is a creativity how-to for leaders. It shows us not only how to get to a creative solution but how to have fun in the process. I endorse this book heartily for all leaders."

—ANN RHOADES, CEO of People Ink and board
member of JetBlue Airways and P. F. Chang's
Restaurants

"John Dillon has written a work of profound gratitude. *The 20-20 Creativity Solution* creates an atmosphere of openness to what may seem impossible, and resolves into welcoming of the new and unexpected. As John writes in his song, 'New Mexico Moon,' 'Thunderstorm's rolling out over the plains / I can feel the sun shining up through the rain.' For John, storm and sunshine express the abundant immensity of life, into which his gratitude pours and from which his, and our, creativity blossoms—the desert flower."

—MICHAEL SHENKMAN, PhD, business consultant and
author of *The Arch and the Path: The Life of Leading Greatly*

"John Dillon's book, *The 20-20 Creativity Solution*, is an excellent resource for any business leader looking to improve employee engagement. The book takes complex creativity theories and makes them simple and easy to implement in any organization looking to improve creativity and innovation in the workforce. A must-read!"

—DIANNE CRAMPTON, business consultant and author
of *TIGERS Among Us: Winning Business Team Cultures and Why
They Thrive*

The 20-20 Creativity Solution

FOCUS YOUR NATURAL CREATIVITY FOR
SUCCESS, HAPPINESS, AND PEACE OF MIND

John Dillon

Three Creeks
Publishing

Three Creeks Publishing
© 2010 John Dillon

ISBN: 978-0-9845082-4-2
0-9845082-4-4

Grateful acknowledgment is given to reprint material from the
following sources:
Illustration page 57 from *A Whole New Mind*, Daniel Pink (New York:
Penguin 2005) reprinted by permission of the author.

Original artwork credits:
Illustration page 5 "Stylized Brain," Jessica Louise Dillon
Illustration page 33 "Live Performance Energy Flow," Kristin Varner
Illustration page 74 "Inspiration, Action, Analysis," Kristin Varner
Photo on page 119 by Kyle Zimmerman

Cover design by Jessica Louise Dillon
Cover Photo by Kyle Zimmerman
Interior design and typeset by Pamela McGrew

Dedication
To Michael, Jessica, and Jackson,
my proudest creative accomplishments

Contents

About the Author

■ JOHN DILLON has had a fascination with creativity most of his life.

He grew up in a Pennsylvania town that was settled by his Irish immigrant great-great-grandfather, whose son, John's namesake, started a flower-growing business that flourishes to this day. John was given a guitar at age thirteen, and shortly thereafter began playing blues and rock with his teenage bandmates. A major turning point came in his late teens when he discovered firsthand the power of music to build community and transcend severe physical limitations.

Pack on back and guitar in hand, John spent a couple of years crisscrossing the United States, absorbing the landscape and culture of our great country. Eventually he settled in northern New Mexico, where he joined a spiritual community and studied the art of meditation.

He was so passionate about guitars that in his mid-twenties he learned how to build them. He made more than eighty acoustic guitars, including custom instruments for several music stars.

A twelve-year stint in the family floral business gave John the opportunity to apply his creativity to marketing and business. He started a division of the company that sold plants to mass-market outlets and developed a program for importing directly from the flower auction in Aalsmeer, Holland. While in the floral business, he was an active leader in state and national trade associations.

Throughout John's varied vocational endeavors, song-writing and music performance continued to be vital forms of creative expression. He recorded his first solo CD, *Piece of Paradise*, in 1998. His second release, *Callin' Me Home*, which chronicled his return to the West, received seven New Mexico Music Award nominations and one win.

In 2004, John and his wife, Vivian Nesbitt, created the syndicated radio program *Art of the Song: Creativity Radio*, which is now heard by more than 250,000 listeners every week on more than two hundred public and community stations across North America.

John is the proud father of three very creative individuals: Michael, a successful composer and performer of electronic music in Berlin, Germany; Jessica, a student of the arts and the mother of a one-year-old in California; and Jackson, a budding guitar player with his band in Las Vegas.

Gratitude

■ To FAMILY: Dorry and Doug (Mom and Dad) for love and support even when it didn't make sense. To Charles for spiritual leadership, and Rob for sustaining the family legacy. To Michael, Jessica, and Jackson for keeping their creativity alive. To Anna Rubyan, who taught me to appreciate beauty and spirit in a song. To Tory Franklin-Dillon who taught me that all life *is* art.

To all who helped with the publishing of this book: Allegra Huston for editing, Dianne Crampton for encouragement, Karla Eoff for copy editing, Jessica Dillon for cover design, Kyle Zimmerman for cover photography, Kristin Varner and Jessica Dillon for illustrations, and Pamela McGrew for typesetting and layout. To Mark Victor Hansen for telling me to write first then do the research, and that if the message came from my heart, it would have value. To the core group of 20-20 practitioners who showed me through their dedication and experience that this book could indeed have a positive impact: Jean Balliet, Kelly and Michael Barrett, Christina Bouajila, Anne Carley, Tania Casselle, Beth DeSombre, Rick Drost, Karen Gault, David

Gray, Allegra Huston, Sally LaFaver, Cathy Main, Kristine Maltrud, Tish and Mike Miller, Carol Morgan-Eagle, James Navé, Tim Nenninger, Brian Quinn, Jesse White, and Betty Widerski.

To friends of *Art of the Song*: Mike Tilley for the idea; Tim Nenninger for production assistance, organization, and enthusiasm; Michael Shorr for being the Song Analyst; and Don Richmond for his frequent Creativity Corner essays. To all the program directors who took the risk to put us on the air, especially early adopters Abby Goldstein, Wayne Mohr, Deb Nichols, and Brian Quinn. To Steve Rathe and Matthew Payne at Murray Street Marketing, and Kathy Gronau and the team at Creative PR for marketing. To Lee and Susan Berk, Martin Chavez, Tom Frouge, Rob Hayes, Peter Mitchell, and all *Art of the Song* members and contributors for financial support. To Dean Mark Goodman, Ken and Cindy Davis, Dick Forbes, Jane Gober, and all the folks at St. John's Episcopal Cathedral for *A Creative Spirit* and office space. To D. D. Wigley for living space. To John Burgund, Tristan Clum, Matthew Finch, Roman Garcia, Richard Towne, and all the folks at KUNM.

To my teachers and mentors in spirit and life: Diana and Robert van Arsdale, Bill Baker, Lama Karma Chodrak, Craig Duswalt, Jim Folkman, Fred Fries, Bill Hidlay, Leslie Hoffman, Charlie Howe, Max Krimmel, Canon Kermit Lloyd, Dwight Lund, Herman Rednick, Michael Shenkman, Bob Tevis, and Lynn Trojahn.

To my music buds: Scott Bennett, Charles Dillon,

Francis Donald, Jonathan and Deborah Hutchison, Tim Long, Tom Naunas, Rod Phillips, and Mark Tomeo.

To my cosmic hide-and-seek pals: Jeff Algatt, Bill Brobst, Steve Coval, Sue Fullmer, Ray Ghelardi, Jonathan Hutchison, Jeff Jones, Tom Naunas, Stan Reed, and John Scrip.

And especially to my wife, Vivian, for loving, encouraging, and bringing out the best in me...always.

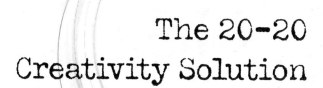

The 20-20
Creativity Solution

1

What's So Important About Creativity?

the **quest** for **creativity** is not about searching
for some **mysterious** thing outside of ourselves.
it's about relaxing—revealing and removing the
blocks that stand in the way—and gently letting our
AUTHENTIC SELVES express in the world

■ "WE ALL HAVE A SONG TO SING…and we hope this program inspires you to sing yours." That's how we close every edition of *Art of the Song: Creativity Radio*. Indeed, there is a song in every one of us—a creative genius that wants to express itself. Creativity is not reserved for artists, musicians, writers, and dancers; it is available to all of us. Maybe your reaction is: "Of course, that's a no-brainer." Maybe you're thinking: "No way, are you kidding? I'm not creative." Or maybe you're somewhere in the middle: "That's a nice idea, but how do I access my creativity?"

If you are in the "no way" camp, I urge you to read on. I will present evidence to support my claim, and I will show you how accessing your inner creativity can make you more successful at work and in your personal life, increase your levels of happiness, and ultimately improve your health. I'll present easy-to-use tools and strategies that will help you experience firsthand this amazing resource that's inside you.

If you are among the "already believers" or "somewhere in the middles," I hope to shed new insight on your creative process and offer some new techniques for accessing your creativity more of the time. Of course, you too will add more happiness, effectiveness, and bodily health if you apply the practice and principles presented in this book.

In my "20-20 Creativity Solution" multimedia presentations (information available at ArtoftheSong.com) I start out by asking the audience, "How many of you consider yourselves to be creative?" Usually less than half of the people raise their hands. Then I ask, "How many of you have ever had a thought, and then found a dozen or so words and spoke them together in a sentence that expressed that thought?" Invariably all raise their hands. Creating a sentence in this way is the essence of the creative process, and we all do it hundreds of times every day. You'll see how this conforms to the definition of creativity in Chapter 4.

Creative expression is easier and more natural than you may think. It is your birthright. It's what it means to be human. You are an infinitely creative being at the core, and this is who you really are—your Authentic Self. Throughout this book I'll use the term "Authentic Self" to refer to the higher or spiritual self, the true self, the soul, the part of you that is eternal and infinitely creative. The purpose of this book is to help you tap into that naturally creative part of yourself in order to live a balanced and successful life.

Most of us have been trained by our schooling and social conditioning to be very effective analytical thinkers. With this focus, however, it's easy to forget something: imagination and creativity. Most schools, particularly in the public education system, discourage these little-understood qualities and disparage them with terms like "daydreaming," "head in the clouds," or "not paying attention." There are some good schools that take a more balanced approach to education, but many of us are afflicted by this imbalance toward the analytical way of thinking.

Your Authentic Self

YOU have access to infinite creativity
YOU have **all** the answers
YOU are happiness and fulfillment
YOU are a **DIVINE CREATIVE** being!

EVERYDAY CREATIVITY

In an interview in the December 2009 issue of *Psychology Today*, Michelle Root-Bernstein said, "It's too bad that when considering what endeavors may be creative, people immediately think of the arts...Just about anything can be addressed in a creative manner, from housecleaning to personal hobbies to work."

In that light, let's talk about "everyday creativity." If you don't consider yourself to be an artist, musician, writer, or dancer, do you enjoy cooking? Do you enjoy picking out what you're going to wear for the day? What about doing projects with your kids or grandkids? Making a scrapbook? Do you enjoy an intimate conversation, or telling a good story? How about tending houseplants or a garden? Rearranging the furniture or decorating your home? Writing a letter or something in your journal? You get the idea. There are hundreds of ways you express your unique vision in the world every day. If you approach your daily activities with mindfulness and awareness, you bring a spirit of creativity to all that you do. Be open to inspiration, and allow your intuition to guide you. The point is to view everything as a creative act. Look at each day as a brand-new canvas on which to paint a work of art. All it takes is a new perspective—to look at the world with 20-20 vision.

A BRAIN DIVIDED

The human brain is an extremely complex organ consisting of billions of cells. In addition to thinking and cognitive abilities, the brain controls—below our level of awareness—

all the functions of the body that keep us alive and healthy. I choose not to go too deeply into the physiology of the brain here, and will focus mainly on the concepts relevant to our understanding of the creative process.

The brain is divided into two hemispheres—the left and the right. They are connected by the corpus callosum, which transmits information back and forth between the two. The right hemisphere controls the left side of the body, and the left hemisphere controls the right side of the body. This is why if someone has a stroke in the left hemisphere, the right side of the body becomes impaired, and vice versa.

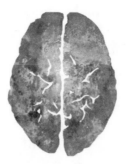

Artist's Representation of the Brain

In the 1970s, Nobel laureate Roger Sperry performed significant research by severing the corpus callosum of epileptic patients, thereby isolating and identifying the functions of each hemisphere. He wrote, "There appear to be two modes of thinking, verbal and nonverbal, represented rather separately in left and right brain hemispheres, respectively..." The two hemispheres serve very different functions and work simultaneously to gather and process information. One way to describe how the two hemispheres work is to say that the right side looks at the big picture and the left side handles the details. Throughout the course of a day we use the right brain and left brain together in varying proportions. Because of our unique environmental and cultural backgrounds, most of us tend to be dominant in one hemisphere or the other. In the United States, more than 90 percent of the population are left-brain dominant. It's interesting to note that Asian cultures are generally more right-brain dominant than Western cultures.

Let's look at how each brain hemisphere functions.

THE RIGHT HEMISPHERE: INTUITIVE

The "big picture" thinking right hemisphere actually does think in pictures. It takes in information from all our senses—sight, sound, smell, taste, touch—and forms a sensory collage of the present moment. Inspiration, intuition, imagination, and insight all come through the right hemisphere. The right brain is the part of us that experiences joy, and a connection to others and to a power greater than ourselves—functions of being in the present moment. When people meditate by quieting the mind (left brain)—thereby eliminating thoughts of past and future—it is this present-moment connection of the right hemisphere that often opens them to a spiritual experience. In *My Stroke of Insight*, neuroscientist Jill Bolte Taylor, PhD, chronicles her left-hemisphere stroke and subsequent recovery. She speaks from firsthand experience when she describes living almost entirely in her right brain: "[My] right mind is open to the eternal flow whereby I exist at *one* with the universe. It is the seat of my divine mind." She goes on to say, "[The right mind] understands that we are all connected to one another in an intricate fabric of the cosmos..."

To better understand these human and spiritual connections, I like to use the metaphor of the ocean. Each of us is like an individual wave on the surface of the ocean. No two waves are exactly the same, yet we are all water, all connected as a part of the great ocean. In a similar way, at a consciousness level we are all part of a great power—God, spirit, universe, field of potential, or any name you choose—and through it we are connected with all of humanity. When we are able to quiet the left brain, as in meditation or at a good concert, the right hemisphere of the brain allows us to feel and know this connection at a deep level.

Here are some words and terms that show how the right brain works: abstract, random, synthesis, connection, higher power, present moment, spirit, empathic, compassionate, heart, context, story. As it continually lives in the present, the right brain has no sense of time. No doubt you've heard of super-creative types who are always late for appointments.

THE LEFT HEMISPHERE: RATIONAL

The left hemisphere is the rational-thinking part of the brain. It is great at organizing and categorizing the information that comes in through the right hemisphere. It takes all those wonderfully pictured present moments and strings them together in sequence, thereby creating a sense of time—past, present, and future. The left is the deductive-reasoning part of the brain: If X is true and Y is true, then Z must follow. The processing of language—how letters make words and words make sentences—is a left-brain function, however, it's the right brain that deals with the meaning and the overall concept of what's being said. As Daniel Pink writes in *A Whole New Mind*, the left brain deals with *text* and the right brain deals with *context*.

Judgment occurs in the left hemisphere. Our left brain evaluates any given situation as good or bad based upon the beliefs stored in our memory, then stores our interpretations of experiences, categorized as good or bad. This judging part of ourselves continually compares us to others and assesses how we measure up. This ego mind sees us as separate from others. It is the critical voice in our heads that may sometimes get in the way of the creative process. As you'll see in Chapter 4, however, the left hemisphere also contributes a valuable and necessary element in the creative process. The left hemisphere is truly an amazing instrument. It should be respected, nurtured, and used to the fullest, but it should not be in control of our lives.

Here are some words that describe the function of the left hemisphere: logical, linear, analysis, separate, ego, time, self, mind, numbers, text, facts.

This chart summarizes the ways the two hemispheres of the brain process information:

Left Hemisphere	Right Hemisphere
Rational	Intuitive
Logical	Abstract
Linear	Random
Analysis	Synthesis
Separate	Connected
Individual	Community
Ego	Spirit
Text	Context
Verbal	Nonverbal
Judgmental	Empathic
Calculating	Compassionate
Masculine	Feminine
Facts	Story
Mind	Heart
Past and Future	Present Moment

WE HAVE A CHOICE

Are you spending enough time in the *right* hemisphere of your brain—the part that ignites the fire of creativity, inspiration, intuition, and insight? Author and wealth expert David Cameron Gikandi says that we only need to spend about 10 percent of our time in the left hemisphere—the "rational thinking" part of our brain. The other 90 percent of our time, he says, should be spent in an open and receptive (right-brain) state. But as you'll see in the coming chapters, our culture has educated most of us to live predominantly in the left hemisphere of our brains.

I'm not suggesting that we go as extreme as Mr. Gikandi advocates, but 50-50 would be a nice improvement. And perhaps we might want to rethink which side is in the driver's seat. Maybe they have it right in England, where the driver sits on the right side.

Imagine for a moment a tree that gets all the water and nutrients it needs but only a small percentage of the sunshine required for sustenance. This tree would likely suffer from some kind of ill health or disease. A person locked in the left-brain analytical way of thinking and using intuition only upon occasion is like the tree that is getting plenty of water but is trying to survive on a fraction of its required sunlight. Just like the tree needs sunshine, we all need creative nourishment.

ART OF THE SONG

I'd like to tell the story of how the public radio program *Art of the Song* was created and how it evolved during its first six years. I share this to demonstrate how I've acquired a deep passion for creative exploration, as well as to illustrate my belief that entrepreneurship is one of the highest—and perhaps most challenging—forms of creativity. It was through our work with *Art of the Song* that the seeds for this book were sown.

In 2003, my wife, Vivian Nesbitt, and I were touring the country as folksingers, playing in coffeehouses, churches, and house concerts. One day we ran into our friend Mike Tilley, who worked at the local community radio station, and he said, "You guys should think about doing a radio show, maybe a short segment about what it's like to be musicians on the road." It sounded like a nice idea—particularly since I had produced and hosted a program on a college radio station a few years back. Life went on and we never acted on it. Six months later we received a call from Mike, and he asked if we had thought about his idea of doing a radio show. We said that we were interested. He said, "Well, you need to put a proposal together because one of our programs was canceled, and we're looking to fill the slot." Hmmm, we thought, opportunity rarely knocks twice, and maybe we should do this. "Okay, we'll think about it," we said to Mike, to which he said, "You better think fast, because the program committee meets in one hour." Viv and I bounced a few ideas around and called back with our proposal to do a one-hour music-and-interview program about songwriting. The program director agreed to give us one hour once a month.

So it began. We started *Art of the Song* by interviewing all the songwriters we knew—and we did know quite a few from being in the music business and through my career as a guitar maker. We broadened our horizons by attending folk festivals and music conferences, interviewing the performers there.

Somewhere along the way, it occurred to us that if we could do *Art of the Song* well on one station, why couldn't we get the show on hundreds of stations across the country? And, if each station paid us a few bucks a show, we might even be able to earn a living doing something that we really loved. What a concept! Little did we know that (a) stations didn't normally pay for independently produced programs, and (b) it would be a hard sell just to get the stations to *give* us one hour of airtime. But we didn't let this stop us because we loved producing the show and it was fun, rewarding work.

As we interviewed more and more songwriters, we noticed that most of them spoke very passionately about their process—almost as a kind of spiritual experience. We realized that many of the concepts they were talking about were universal and could be applied to other forms of artistic expression, such as painting, writing, and dancing, as well as to everyday creative acts like cooking a meal and raising a family.

Around this same time we began to realize that a radio show with a narrow focus on songwriting would likely have a very limited audience—specifically, other songwriters and musicians. This might present a problem when we tried to convince stations to give us an hour of airtime. We knew *Art of the Song* would be doomed before leaving the gate if we didn't broaden the potential audience. I woke up one morning—you know, in that time when you're half awake and half asleep—with the idea that we should add a short segment to the show and call it the Creativity Corner. This would be a spoken essay on the general topic of creativity from an artist or creative professional. We would further broaden the show's appeal by posing more general questions about creativity to our guests.

Also around this time another friend, writer Deonne Kahler, asked if we had ever heard of creativity coach Eric Maisel. We hadn't, and she recommended one of his books, *Coaching the Artist Within*. We read it, and immediately phoned Eric and asked if we could interview him for the Creativity Corner. That was the beginning of a fine friendship and working partnership. Not only did he become a regular contributor to the Creativity Corner but together we founded TeleSummits.com, a provider of creativity education through telephone conference calls and audio downloads.

With insatiable curiosity, we started reading every book

we could get our hands on that had anything to do with creativity. We discovered other authors, including Paul Ray, Julia Cameron, Daniel Pink, Matthew Fox, Richard Florida, Mihaly Csikszentmihalyi, and Sir Ken Robinson—to name a few. We were pleasantly surprised by the number of books available on the subject of creativity (see the Recommended Reading and Resources section for all of our faves). What we learned was very encouraging with regard to audience development. We learned that *everyone* has the capacity to be creative; it is one of the things that separates humans from other living beings. We also learned that many people didn't particularly think of themselves as creative, that there was a persistent delusion that creativity is just for artists, musicians, writers, and dancers—the "gifted" ones. We discovered that engaging in a creative activity has many beneficial effects with regard to health and well-being, both for the individual and for society as a whole, and that there is a relationship between creativity and spirituality. In addition, we learned that there are many ways creativity can be put to good use in business, and that cities with a strong culture of creativity reap substantial economic rewards.

Thus, our mission was born: *Through talking with songwriters and other creative people we inspire listeners to express themselves creatively, and we dispel the myth that some people are not creative.*

With all this research and little more than a handful of experience under our belts, we hired a New York public radio marketing firm to help us launch nationally. The first thing Murray Street Marketing did was send recordings of the show out to five program directors for review. This was truly a humbling experience. One thought the show was okay, a few tore it apart, and one thought it was a joke. We were told in so many words that creativity is too broad a topic, too conceptual. "You can't talk about creativity on the radio," some said. We were shattered. Quite honestly, we were ready to give up the silly notion that we could be successful radio producers on a national level. After about the third day, we picked ourselves up off the floor and decided that we could make *some* of the recommended changes—get a new theme song, get voice training (me), and improve our interviewing and editing skills—while keeping the core mission of exploring creativity intact. We made those changes, got a new theme song from Darrell Scott, a well-respected Nashville writer, and launched nationally in January 2005.

We reached our goal of fifty stations the first year. At the time of this writing *Art of the Song* is on more than two hundred stations. (See ArtoftheSong.org/stations for a list and a map.) Our strong foundation of 250,000 weekly listeners is a diverse group with various means of expressing themselves creatively. We receive financial support from Berklee College of Music in Boston, the city of Albuquerque, and other organizations and individuals who believe in the power of creativity. The fact that we've shown remarkable growth in the first six years demonstrates that we're tapping into an ever-growing community of professional and "everyday" creatives, proving that creativity *is* an important topic that has broad interest.

THE ECONOMICS OF CREATIVITY

Creativity is good for business and good for the economy. Recently Vivian and I made a presentation at an international conference on "creative tourism" that was sponsored by the United Nations organization UNESCO. The conference was attended by representatives from cities from around the world who recognized the value in cultivating cultures of creativity to attract tourism. The underlying principle of the conference was that when recognized and promoted properly, creativity—as manifested in the art, craft, music, and culture of a place—acts as a magnet for tourists, which yields significant economic benefits to a city, state, or country.

As of 2002, more than thirty-eight million Americans made their living in a creative or related field, according to Richard Florida in his book *The Rise of the Creative Class*. Florida believes that the creative class is rapidly becoming the driving force in our economy. If our society is to thrive, we must nurture creativity in our emerging workforce. It's no wonder that Jonathan Feinstein's class on creativity in business is one of the most popular at the Yale School of Management. According to Feinstein, major corporations are now recruiting managers who actively pursue their outside interests in music or art. What this means is that there are an increasing number of employment opportunities for people like you and me who are actively developing creative skills.

HAPPINESS AND SUCCESS

happiness is not in the mere possession of money. It lies in the joy of ACHIEVEMENT, in the thrill of **creative effort**
—FRANKLIN D. ROOSEVELT

There are significant benefits to be enjoyed through expressing our creative voices, many of which are by-products of accessing our Authentic Selves. Engaging in a creative activity—when we become truly lost in the flow—puts us in harmony with our Authentic Selves, our spiritual nature. This connects us with a life force that has the power to transform when we follow its guidance and go with the flow. Creative exploration, whether it is in the arts or of the everyday variety, can generate a sense of meaning and purpose in our lives, a knowledge that we're making a difference in the world. This leads to a feeling of satisfaction and, thus, a reduction of anxiety. Creativity can actually aid in bringing a person out of depression, which is often the result of unexpressed creativity.

You will learn in Chapter 4 that creativity is a holistic experience, involving the use of mind, body, and spirit. In *The Ultimate Happiness Prescription*, Deepak Chopra says, "When mind, body, and spirit are in harmony, happiness is the natural result." Using my trusty left-brain deductive reasoning, it follows that happiness would be the result of engaging in the creative process. Further, when we express creativity we engage the right hemisphere of the brain, which is the part that lives in the present moment, the part that allows us to recognize our connection to spirit and to humanity as a whole. When we are aware of our connectedness to spirit and others, we know that we are not alone. These present-moment connections bring a sense of happiness and joy. In *Promoting Health Through Creativity*, Therese Schmid says, "Creativity is an innate capacity in humans which, when expressed through everyday activities, has a major impact on health and well-being." When we're healthy, spiritually connected, and feeling good about ourselves, we experience true happiness.

Like individuals, organizations need creativity manifesting as innovation to survive and prosper. First of all, if you are able to apply creativity in your job you'll likely be happier and more positive at work. People will enjoy working with you. A recent survey indicates that the people most satisfied with their jobs are either working in a creative or a helping profession, both of which require the use of right-brain skills. Second, if you regularly use creativity to generate new ideas and contribute to the success of your organization, you probably won't be receiving a pink slip anytime soon. Those of us who truly develop our creative abilities will be in demand by employers, as these skills cannot easily be outsourced. Whether you work for someone else or own your own business, increasing your "creativity quotient" will translate into greater success.

I've had a variety of jobs over the years. What looks like,

at first glance, a disconnected jumble of occupations is actually connected by the common thread of creativity. I started as an electrician, a seemingly left-brain occupation of running wires in a very linear fashion and a very logical sequence. But scratch the surface, and you'll see that an electrician actually takes intense and potentially dangerous electrical energy and channels it (through wires) into usefulness, enabling lights to light, ovens to cook, and motors to spin—not unlike the way an artist takes the very powerful spiritual energy of creativity and channels it into a work of art. While working by day as an electrician, I played guitar and wrote songs at night.

In 1975, I learned how to build guitars from a talented craftsman and artist, Max Krimmel. He taught me the value of trusting my intuition when it came to planing and sanding the top wood and shaving the braces to achieve the perfect sound. I honed my skills, developed my own intuitive abilities, and ended up building more than eighty guitars. Some were my own design and many were custom-built to help well-known artists better express their creativity.

Sandwiched in the middle of my guitar-making career, I spent some time as a marketing executive in my family's fourth-generation wholesale floral business. I had a legacy to explore. In 1875, my great-grandfather John Lloyd Dillon started a business of growing flowers and selling them to florists throughout northeastern Pennsylvania. My grandfather and father subsequently nurtured and grew the business into one of the largest and most successful rose growers in the eastern United States. Having grown up in the family business and being named after its founder, I  wanted to explore my heritage. At Dillon Floral, I was able to use my creativity to develop marketing programs and establish a new corporate division. The overall mission of the company was to provide fresh flowers and floral products to enable floral designers to better express their creativity. After twelve years in the business (and a serious midlife crisis!), it became clear that I needed to nourish my soul by doing creative work more directly, and I returned to full-time songwriting and guitar making.

After several years, I moved back to New Mexico, met and married Vivian, and you just read the *Art of the Song* story.

In summary, I've followed a career path of exploring my own creativity and crafting tools to enhance people's creative expression. Whether it was a handmade custom guitar for a Nashville songwriter, creating new product lines and marketing systems for the family floral business, or serving 250,000 listeners a week with inspiring radio programming, my mission to express and support creativity has been at the core of my work for more than thirty-five years.

PERSONAL TRANSFORMATION

When people think of the artistic process they usually think of the value being in the product created. For example, a painter creates paintings that are sold in a gallery, sometimes for a lot of money. A novelist writes a book that ends up on the shelves at Barnes & Noble and Borders, and before long it hits the national bestseller list. A hit songwriter may write a song that gets cut by Garth Brooks and sells a million copies. The value is in the product, right?

But what about the Tibetan monks who spend weeks creating a beautiful sand mandala only to destroy it, and reverently pour the sand into a river three days after their painstaking work is finished? Artist Victoria Franklin-Dillon (my former wife) is known for her outdoor sculptures with layers of different colors of adobe (dried mud), which will naturally erode, change colors, and eventually disappear back into the earth. She often does performance-art pieces associated with her sculptures. These performances only happen once; if you weren't there, you missed it. And what about the many songwriters, poets, and artists who create for the pure joy of creating, never expecting to sell their work?

While there is definitely value in the *product*, I'd like to suggest that there is equal or perhaps greater value in the actual *process* of the creation, because the process literally transforms the artist (and in many cases, the audience as well). The experience of creating something allows the artist to tap into the universal flow, and this lifeblood energy is indeed a transforming power.

while there is definitely value in the **product**... there is equal or perhaps greater VALUE in the actual **process** of the CREATION

KEY POINTS

I. You don't have to be an artist, musician, writer, or dancer to enjoy the benefits of creativity. Creativity is something you can access and use in your everyday life.

2. The brain is divided into two hemispheres that work simultaneously but in different ways to process information. The right hemisphere functions in an intuitive, big-picture way. It is the receiver and synthesizer of ideas. The left hemisphere functions in a rational, detail-oriented way. It organizes and analyzes information.

3. Creativity can contribute to happiness and success at home and at work.

4. Creativity can be a powerful agent for personal transformation. The *process* of creating may be as important as the *product* that is created.

ACTION STEPS

I. Start a creativity journal. Nothing fancy. A spiral notebook will do. Use it to write down any insights

or aha moments you have as you read this book.
Feel free to write down anything you want in this
journal. You might think of it as carrying on a
dialogue with the creative part of yourself.

2. As you go through your day, notice the things you
   do that could be considered "creative," even if you
   didn't think of them as creative before. Just raise
   your sense of awareness or mindfulness as you
   go through your day. Say to yourself, "How am I
   bringing my unique vision into the day?" Do this
   in both your work and your personal life. Write
   your insights in your creativity journal.

3. Take a look at the chart on page 9, and for each row
   ask yourself which type of thinking you generally
   gravitate toward. Make a check mark next to the one
   that resonates more for you. Tally up the marks and
   see which column has more checks. This will give
   you an idea of whether you are right- or left-brain
   dominant.

4. At the end of the day, write in your creativity
   journal about the newfound creativity in your life.

2

What Is Creativity?

> **creativity** is to engage in UNIVERSAL FLOW,
> and having some sort of relationship with that.
> to me creativity is my WILLINGNESS to **step up**
> to the plate and take action that will reflect some
> sort of **connectedness** to that larger flow.
> —JAMES NAVÉ, poet and creativity consultant

MY CREATIVE JOURNEY

I KNEW VERY LITTLE about the creative process in August 1969 when I threw a change of clothes and a sleeping bag into Stan Reed's 1962 Ford Fairlane. The two of us headed north from our Pennsylvania hometown toward a remote farm near Bethel, New York. I had no idea that what was to transpire over the next few days would change my life—forever.

As a child I was very creative. All children are creative. Look at the way they play, the way they make up words and dance, the way they find new uses for objects. Children are virtual fountains of creativity. But then something happens. They begin to hear the word "no," and they are guided—sometimes gently, sometimes not so gently—toward behavior that is socially acceptable. Thus begins the socialization process.

Because of where in the calendar my birthday fell, I started school when I was four and a half. I don't remember it, but my mother tells of how I cried the first day she dropped me off at kindergarten. I was the youngest and smallest in my class throughout elementary school. We sat in rows in alphabetical order, and were taught not to speak out of turn, to color within the lines, and to sing in tune. I remember being reprimanded often for looking out the window, daydreaming. I now know that I was simply exercising my imagination, and in the best of all worlds, that skill would have been encouraged and nurtured.

In December, our third-grade class was preparing to sing for a Christmas presentation. We were all lined up in rows learning our song—something about "Gloria in Ex celsis"—when Mrs. Stickler (yes, that was her name) singled out the boy next to me and told him to just mouth the words because he was singing out of tune. Well, I was such a sensitive child that I took that message to heart and stopped singing as well. "That was scary. Maybe I should be quiet, too. I don't want to risk being called out for singing off-key," I rationalized. This seemingly insignificant event grew over time into a deeply held belief that I'm not a singer, that I don't have a good voice.

School was a hostile environment for a shy child like me. Other kids teased me, and I only had a couple of friends. After school I would take refuge in left-brain hobbies like assembling model airplanes and trains, eventually learning to build walkie-talkies, amplifiers, and other electronic components from kits. I became very good at following instructions. I learned to play the left-brain game well. But what had happened to my creativity?

A few years later I was encouraged to take piano lessons. My mother would take me after school every Tuesday and Friday. Playing piano was fun sometimes, but I wasn't passionate about it. The teacher was somewhat lackluster, and I had little motivation to practice. Terrified at the prospect of going in front of an audience, I decided to quit just before my first recital.

Then, in 1964, something happened. I remember listening to WABC's Cousin Brucie and Scott Muni covering the arrival of the Beatles in New York. Who were these long-haired guys from England? I felt like I was listening to history in the making as I pressed my ear to the transistor radio under my pillow while my parents thought I was sleeping. In my hometown of Bloomsburg, Pennsylvania, WABC's AM daytime signal was too weak to receive, but at night this station would become my audio window into the world of popular culture. Later that week, along with about seventy-four million other Americans, I tuned in to *The Ed Sullivan Show*, and was particularly intrigued by how the girls screamed and fell in love with these guys with guitars. Suddenly it became cool to play guitar. And in that same year, as fate would have it, my aunt gave me an old Stella guitar for my thirteenth birthday. Perhaps it was ego-driven at first, but I was truly motivated to learn guitar! I began by playing along with the Beatles and other British Invasion records and learning a few chords from my cousin Jonathan Hutchison. Eventually Jonathan, my brother Charles, and I got together with a few friends and formed a band. I had found a way to express myself creatively! It made me happy in those uncertain teenage years, because—as I now understand—this creative expression put me in touch with who I really was, my Authentic Self.

The Epitome of Sound, circa 1966, left to right:
Tom Naunas, Charles Dillon, me, Bud Musselman,
Jonathan Hutchison (drums)

In a nutshell, due to the external factors of socialization, peer pressure, and school, I developed my left-brain skills, and my creative abilities faded until their fortunate awakening through music in my teen years. But I still consider myself to be a left-brainer who has to make a conscious effort to express myself creatively. In spite of my ability to flow freely and passionately in the language of a wailing guitar, reclaiming the singing and speaking voice that was lost in the third grade has been a lifelong process. I have talked with many people who had similar experiences in their childhood. Some allowed these events to shut down their creativity and others have said, "Wait a minute, I'm not going to let go of my creativity. It's too important."

Still miles away from that upstate New York farm, Stan and I found ourselves stuck in a traffic jam the likes of which that rural county had never seen. Our only option was to pull the car off the road and walk the rest of the way. Which we did. Huffing and puffing, we reached the entrance to find that the festival promoters had declared Woodstock to be a free concert. There was such a huge crowd that the staff and fences were inadequate to keep people out. I was able to keep my tickets as a souvenir (note the reasonable price!).

Woodstock Music and Art Fair	Woodstock Music and Art Fair	Woodstock Music and Art Fair
FRIDAY	**SATURDAY**	**SUNDAY**
August 15, 1969	August 16, 1969	August 17, 1969
10 A. M.	10 A. M.	10 A. M.
$6.00	**$6.00**	**$6.00**
Good For One Admission Only	Good For One Admission Only	Good For One Admission Only
54104 NO REFUNDS	54104 NO REFUNDS	54104 NO REFUNDS

As we came close to the top of the hill we could hear the soaring voice of Joan Baez floating across the fields. Joining with thousands of music fans—I had no idea that there were so many disenfranchised teenagers like us—we walked together as if toward some yet unknown mecca.

What we experienced over the next three days was nothing short of magic. We became part of the transformation of a vacant farm field into a city of nearly half a million. However, the magic of Woodstock was not in the numbers, not in the fact that it became a free concert, but in what held it together—the glue. And that glue was the music, the creative process in action, connecting musician and audience with a spirit of love and peace, something beyond the physical. I didn't know what it was, but I could feel that something amazing was happening. The result was that in spite of pouring rain, slithery mud, and inadequate infrastructure, there were virtually no instances of violence; people got along. The Woodstock vision, "three days of peace and music," would prevail.

I knew in those three soggy days that I would spend the rest of my life exploring the magic of Woodstock, which I would later come to know as the creative process.

THE MAGIC OF LIVE PERFORMANCE

Okay, so I experienced something amazing at Woodstock, and I'd been wanting to figure out what happened and why it was so powerful for those of us who were there. I knew it had something to do with energy, and I knew it had something to do with spirituality. So I began asking some questions. What is it about the energy flow between artist and audience that seems to transcend the physical? What does energy flow have to do with the creative process? How did the music at Woodstock have the power to build and hold that community of half a million together in a spirit of love and peace?

When we attend a concert or festival there is something going on behind the scenes that we cannot see. I'm not talking about what goes on backstage with the crew, managers, and performers. There is something nonphysical, in the realm of energy and emotion, that engages our senses, uplifts us, and in most cases causes us to leave the event somewhat different than when we arrived. Guitar teacher extraordinaire Jamie Andreas explains it this way: "Music puts us in touch with our intuition, our *inward knowing* of the Spiritual Reality that stands behind this physical one we normally touch." When we are truly engaged in the music of a live performance—whether it be rock, folk, or classical— the left brain becomes quiet as we *lose ourselves* in the music. In this state of creative ecstasy, the right brain allows the recognition of our natural connection to each other and to a spirit greater than ourselves. This explains the sense of community that occurred at Woodstock and that happens at most live events.

Here's what happens from an energy standpoint. The musician or band taps into the universal flow of creativity, as James Navé describes in the quote that opens this chapter. That creative energy is then transmitted to the audience, much like an electrical transformer takes the high-voltage electricity from long-distance transmission lines, steps down the voltage, and distributes it for use in homes and businesses. The audience receives this energy both as sound waves and as spiritual energy. If the music is good and the audience responds with appreciation, the energy is amplified based on the size of the audience and the intensity of their response, and is fed back to the performers. This sets up a circular pattern of creative energy that grows and grows, spiraling upward in intensity throughout the concert, often culminating in a rousing request for an encore.

Live Performance Energy Flow

Art of the Song guest Karen Savoca spoke of this magic as "surrender." Here's what she said in her 2009 interview: "Surrender...to me that's what it's all about. When you get an audience that's willing to surrender to the music, and you get this beautiful flow...you feel like you're in this special community...even if just for a short time. It's a beautiful thing."

The Grateful Dead were magicians of live performance. They spoke of a "seventh" member of the band showing up when the creative spirit was truly present. Grateful Dead concerts were so magical that, although the group sold relatively few records, their stadium concerts were almost always sold out.

Most of us go to concerts for entertainment purposes, and the natural high or spiritual experience is not something we're consciously aware of. I'd like to suggest that when we are truly entertained, we feel enriched and uplifted by the performance because we actually give and receive energy and become connected to something greater than ourselves. As audience members we are actual participants in the creative process. This is what I call *active* entertainment (more about active and passive entertainment in Chapter 6). As it was for me in 1969 and many times since, a live concert can truly be a spiritual experience.

CREATIVE FLOW

We've taken an in-depth look at the creative process from an audience perspective. Now let's look at it from the artist's point of view. Have you ever been so engrossed in a project that you looked up at the clock and thought, "Where did the time go?" You were so involved with what you were doing that time seemed to stand still. This is the creative flow. This is living in the present moment—the domain of the right brain. Past and future don't exist when you're in the right-brain creative flow. It's similar to what happens in meditation. The left brain is quieted and you expand into the infinity of your spirit. It also happens with athletes. Runners, for example, speak of the "runner's high" that happens after they've been running for a long time and lose awareness of everything but the present moment. In the case of extreme physical exercise, there are actual chemicals released in the brain that create a sense of euphoria. I believe this also happens when we are lost in the flow of creativity. It is in these moments of flowing freely that we truly connect with our Authentic Selves.

FIND YOUR AUTHENTIC SELF

When I was a teenager my friends and I would play our own version of hide-and-seek. Sometime after dark we would all get in a car, and I would sit in the back seat with a blindfold on. The driver would take us far out into the country away from our hometown, usually driving for thirty or forty minutes. I'd have no idea what direction we were going or how far from home we were. At some point, the car would be pulled to the side of the road, usually near a remote farm, and I would be instructed to take the blindfold off. I would then get into the driver's seat, and my challenge would be to find the way back home—which I always did. I had a good sense of direction, and a good knowledge of the landscape and back roads of the region, so I would keep driving until I recognized something—a village, a river, or a mountain. Then I would figure out which direction to go. This was a fun game for me, and I'm not sure why I was usually the one to do the seeking. Maybe it was because I was good at the game, and my friends were always amazed when I would find the way home, no matter how hard they tried to get me lost.

we are NOT human beings in **search** of a spiritual EXPERIENCE. we are **spiritual beings** having a human EXPERIENCE
—PIERRE TEILHARD DE CHARDIN, French mystic

I think there is a cosmic game of hide-and-seek that we play as humans. We *are* spiritual beings on an earthly journey, as Teilhard de Chardin says, and the moment we're born we begin to forget our spiritual nature—to gradually pull the blindfold over our eyes. As babies, we live totally in both worlds, but the more we learn about the physical world—and the more we become socialized—the more we lose awareness of the spiritual world from whence we came. We forget that at our core we are *divine creative beings*. There's nothing wrong with the forgetting; it's part of what it means to be human. You can't play hide-and-seek without first getting lost, that is, becoming hidden from your spiritual nature.

At some point in our lives, however, we start to notice that something is missing. Clues begin to show up to remind us of our spiritual nature: an intense feeling when viewing a great work of art, listening to an incredible jazz solo or violin concerto, or watching an amazing sunset over the ocean or desert. They could be in a book, in a radio program, or in a conversation with a friend. Somehow we feel we are being tugged in a new direction. This is the part where we take the blindfold off and begin the challenge of finding our way home.

Sometimes the need to change direction shows up in a more painful way. At some point it becomes very clear that our lives are not working, and we have no choice but to change. This happened to me seventeen years ago when I "bottomed out" as an alcoholic. My life had gotten so out of control that my only option was to seek help and seriously commit to a twelve-step program (for which I am now very grateful). It was through the twelve-step work that I began my journey home. Fortunate to have a creative outlet back then, I discovered that playing guitar and writing songs allowed me to connect with a deeper part of myself. I came to realize that the creative process was indeed a way to access my spiritual nature, and for me creativity became the key to my spiritual growth—and my sanity.

Many of us are somewhere between the forgetting and the remembering. We may have had glimpses of our Authentic Selves from time to time. The cool thing is that the more often we have these heightened experiences, the closer we get to expressing our Authentic Selves in everything we do. The ultimate goal of the earthly human journey is to rediscover that we really are *divine creative beings*, to *know* it at a deep level, and to *live* it every day.

There are many ways to find our way back home to our Authentic Selves—many paths to the mountaintop, as my teacher Herman Rednick used to say. The way home can be found through organized religion, or through yoga or meditation. Some people find it in nature, some through the discipline of physical exercise. It doesn't matter what path or paths we choose. The purpose of this book is to show how creativity can be a doorway to our Authentic Selves. It can be used by itself or in conjunction with other methods. Learning and pursuing a creative discipline—and facing the fears and working through the blocks that come up—can assist us in doing the work we need to do to awaken us to that spiritual part of ourselves. (I recommend exploring creativity in conjunction with the 20-20 Practice that you'll learn about in Chapter 5.)

Creativity can be a vehicle to deepen the journey home, and a way to know that we're moving in the right direction. The better we become at expressing ourselves creatively, and the more we are able to *lose ourselves* (left-brain ego selves) in the timelessness of creative flow, the more we tap into the creative genius within that *is* the Authentic Self. Step by step we move closer to a place where we're consciously living in both worlds—the spiritual and the physical—at the same time. This is when we get our 20-20 vision back.

TRANSFORM LIMITING BELIEFS

So what specifically do we need to do to reveal our creative Authentic Selves? What is it that prevents us from living in the spiritual and physical worlds at the same time? As I said earlier, when we're babies we live in both worlds simultaneously, but we begin to forget our spiritual nature as we grow up and become socialized. Things happen to us and around us; we experience life. We tell ourselves *stories* about our life experiences, and we form *beliefs* that, over time, we come to accept as *truth*. Here's the important distinction: *It's not the experiences we have but the stories we tell ourselves (and others) about those experiences that form our beliefs, and therefore what we accept as truth*. It works like this:

event ⇨ story ⇨ belief ⇨ truth

These truths, which arise from our stories and beliefs, are usually very different from *universal* Truth. (I'll distinguish between the two through the use of a lowercase "t" for little truth, and capital "T" for universal Truth.) It's the incongruity between what we think is true and Truth that prevents us from living in both the physical and the spiritual world at the same time, and therefore expressing our creative Authentic Selves every day. Said another way, there becomes a disconnect between our reality and spiritual Reality. This disconnect creates and perpetuates the illusion that we are separate from one another and not connected to a higher power. It's the hide-and-seek blindfold we create that obscures our 20-20 spiritual vision as we move through childhood into adulthood.

We create—and therefore must accept full responsibility for—our stories, beliefs, and, ultimately, the blindfold. This is a good thing, because if we created the blindfold, we can remove it, too. Accepting this responsibility is the first step in changing direction and finding the way back home.

We buy into our little truths at such a deep level that we tend to attract and associate with people who share our beliefs. This further entrenches us in the illusion that our beliefs are real. We join groups and political parties that support our beliefs, even watch news networks and listen to radio stations that reinforce these beliefs. The more we buy into our little truths, the more difficult it is to see the Truth.

Our physical world is polarized, dualistic: left or right, rich or poor, city or country, Democrat or Republican, male or female, us or them. You get the idea. The spiritual world is not polarized. At a spiritual level we are all divine creative and eternal beings. Let's look at the creation myth of Adam and Eve. They were part of the spiritual world, shameless, naked, and beautiful, until the thing with the apple. Then they became separate from God, and separate from each other. Thus began the world of duality. On a human level, as babies we are born out of the spiritual world, not knowing separation. As we grow through childhood experiences, we create limiting beliefs, buy into the dualism, and gradually lose sight of the Truth. Life goes on until we wake up one day, start taking off the blindfold, and begin the journey back home. When we reconnect with Truth and become fully integrated with our Authentic Selves, we actually rise above the dualism, and we have the option of choosing not to participate in the polarized world.

Here's an example of the event-story-belief-truth continuum: Suppose a child keeps hearing the message from a parent or teacher that he shouldn't speak unless spoken to. As that message is repeated and reinforced through punishment and discipline, the child tells himself the story "People don't care what I have to say." Eventually the child *believes* the story and comes to accept as *truth* "What I have to say doesn't matter." This is very different from the universal Truth that we all matter and have an important gift to give the world.

Another example: A young girl asks her mother for a new dress, and the mother says something like, "Money doesn't grow on trees." She asks her father for an ice-cream cone and he says, "Honey, we can't afford extras right now." The girl creates a story that she lives in a world where her wants and desires are not met. Eventually she *believes* the story and comes to accept as *truth* that the world is not abundant. Her poverty mentality is not congruent with the universal Truth that the world *is* naturally abundant.

One more example: A white man lives in the turbulent and racially divided society of the 1960s. This man—through what he has been taught and through what he has seen around him—believes that white people are superior to blacks. The Truth is that all human beings are equal in the eyes of the Divine. As long as this man holds the belief that whites are superior to blacks, his beliefs are in conflict with and thus prevent him from seeing the Truth and expressing his Authentic Self.

The good news is that we can change our beliefs and bring them into alignment with universal Truth. We may not be able to change the events that happened in our lives, but we *can* change the stories we tell ourselves about those events. We can dump the old stories from our internal hard drives and replace them with stories that support us on our journey home. The new stories will create new beliefs that are aligned with Truth. When we are aligned with universal Truth, we express our Authentic Selves. As we reconcile the differences between our little truths and Truth, we begin to live a life of integrity. Our 20-20 vision returns.

"Okay, so how do I transform my old beliefs?" you're probably wondering. The first step is to become aware of them. Take an objective look into your childhood experiences and past conditioning and ask yourself, "What do I believe to be true that might not actually be the Truth?" Another good question to ask is: "If the Truth of who I am is eternal, naturally creative, and abundant, what are some of my beliefs that might contradict this Truth?" You might want to consider working with a certified hypnotherapist to help you uncover your limiting beliefs. The interesting thing is that as you begin to express yourself creatively—and as you begin using the 20-20 Practice, which you will soon learn about—many of these old beliefs will naturally appear so that you can transform them.

Once you've identified a limiting belief, the next step is to dissolve it through the use of an affirmation—that is, through positive self-talk. If one of your beliefs is "I'm not a good singer" and you have a sincere desire to sing, repeat to yourself often something like "I have a strong voice, and I always sing on key." Write out your affirmation on a few Post-it notes or 3x5 cards and place them where you'll see them during the day. Repeat the affirmation often, both aloud and silently. After you've identified the limiting belief and begun using an affirmation—and this is the important part—take *action* to reaffirm the Truth. Sign up for a voice lesson!

A word about affirmations: You may be thinking, "Isn't it dishonest to use an affirmation if it isn't true? I'm *not* a great singer with a strong voice." Well, the truth is, if you have a deep desire in your heart, that desire is actually your Authentic Self speaking to you and urging you to be the best that you can be. If you have a true desire—not just a passing thought like "I want a million dollars" but a sincere heartfelt desire like "I have a deep desire to be a millionaire so that I can support my family well and do good in the world"—then you have the ability to fulfill that desire. Notice the difference. The first is merely wanting a thing; the second is desiring to be the kind of person it takes to achieve something great. The Authentic Self doesn't give us desires that can't be fulfilled. If created in alignment with a sincere desire, an affirmation already *is* true from the perspective of your Authentic Self. I like to think of an affirmation as my Authentic Self calling to me from somewhere in the future, saying, "You can do it! You can do it!"

One of my limiting beliefs was that people wouldn't like me if I was successful and had money. This came from growing up in a small town in a family that owned a successful business. Many of my classmates in elementary school teased me about being "rich." It made me feel like something was wrong with me, that I was unlikable because I came from a family that had money. After years of affirmations and hours of therapy, I've finally transformed that limiting belief, and I'm beginning to experience true financial success.

To use the age-old onion analogy, as we peel away the outer layers (our beliefs about what we think is true), eventually we reveal our Authentic Selves and come to know the Truth. The more we reveal our Authentic Selves, the more our natural creativity flows out into the world.

Here's a little affi-rhythm (an affirmation with rhythm and melody, a term coined by singer/songwriter Terry Garthwaite) that I created to express the concept. I sing it to myself often:

I am an eternal being
On an awesome earthly journey
Success is my birthright
And I'm naturally creative
As I peel away the layers, I find the Truth of who I am
Yes, I peel away the layers and find the Truth of who I am

Feel free to sing this one or make up one of your own. Affi-rhythms are a very effective way to transform your old beliefs.

I'll close this chapter with the lyrics to one of my songs that expresses the concept of the cosmic game of hide-and-seek, "Fast Movin' Train." I wrote the song after reading the book *Dancing the Dream*, by Jamie Sams.

Before we came to this earthly life
We knew we were part of something grand
We chose a path and a place to be born
To play our part in a perfect plan

We were born into this world of illusion
Born into this world of pain
Born into this life to learn a thing or two
But forgot about the perfect plan

Spirit voice—into flesh and bone
I feel like I'm a long way from home
World of illusion, world of pain
This life is like a fast movin' train

We forgot we are woven like a tapestry
With each other and every man
Forgot about the Great Mystery
And we're part of a perfect plan

Forgot about the trees, the rain forests green
Forgot we are one with the land
Forgot about the rivers and the oceans blue
And we're part of a perfect plan

Spirit voice—into flesh and bone
I think I hear you callin' me home
World of illusion, world of pain
This life is like a fast movin' train

But we can pierce the veils of illusion
Weave a path through shifting sand
We can dance the dream and seek the Truth
And remember the perfect plan

Spirit voice—into flesh and bone
I'm on my way back home
World of illusion, world of pain

This life is like a fast movin' train
Rolling on this fast movin' train

A version of this song with Peter Rowan singing guest vocals is found on my CD *Callin' Me Home*. You can find a free audio download of my affi-rhythm and "Fast Movin' Train" at 2020CreativitySolution.com.

the good news is that we can **change** our **beliefs** and bring them into alignment with UNIVERSAL TRUTH

KEY POINTS

I. Most of us have had experiences that have
    either encouraged or discouraged us creatively.
    Whichever message was more dominant tends to
    show up in our beliefs about whether or not we're
    creative.

2. As audience members in a live performance
    situation, we actively participate in the creative
    process. We do this by tapping into the right-
    brain ability to connect with others and a higher
    power, thereby building and strengthening
    community.

3. The cosmic game of hide-and-seek is divided
    into two parts. In the first part, we gradually put
    on a blindfold which hides us from our naturally
    creative selves. In the second part, we notice
    something is missing in our lives, we take off the
    blindfold, and we begin the journey back home.

4. We put the blindfold on by telling ourselves *stories*
    about our life experiences and forming *beliefs* that,
    over time, we come to accept as *truth*. We take the
    blindfold off by changing our limiting beliefs and
    integrating with the Truth of who we are.

ACTION STEPS

1. Look back into your childhood. Were there any times that you remember being encouraged for your creativity? If so, make a list and write a page in your creativity journal about the experience that stands out the most. Were there any events that might have closed your creativity down? If so, make a list and write in your creativity journal about the one that seems most significant.

2. Think about the beliefs you hold to be true. Is there anything you can think of that might not really be True (with a capital "T")? Do you believe that you are creative? Do you believe that you are naturally abundant? Choose one of your limiting beliefs and create an affirmation that contradicts the belief and upholds the Truth of who you really are. Write the affirmation on three Post-it notes and place them where you will see them often (computer, refrigerator, bathroom mirror, etc.). Silently say the affirmation throughout the day. Take an action that affirms your new belief.

3. Go to a concert or live entertainment of some kind. Notice the energy that you feel from the

performer(s). Notice the energy that you feel in yourself and perhaps in the other audience members. Do you feel connected to them? See if you can feel the energy grow as the concert progresses. Try consciously giving energy back to the performer(s). Do you feel differently at the end of the concert than before you went? Why? Write about your experience in your creativity journal.

3

Where Has Our Creativity Gone?

the **intuitive** mind is a **sacred gift** and
the rational mind is a faithful servant.
we have CREATED A SOCIETY that honors the
servant and has FORGOTTEN the gift.
—ALBERT EINSTEIN

THE HISTORY OF HUMAN CREATIVITY

■ THE DICTIONARY defines creativity as *to make or bring into existence something new.*

Creativity began about forty thousand years ago in the Upper Paleolithic period, when our *Homo sapiens* ancestors first created tools out of bone and ivory.[1] Relics from this period offer evidence of the first examples of humans making something that didn't exist before. Early examples

---

1. Roger Lewin, *The Origin of Modern Humans* (New York: Henry Holt and Company, 1998).

of human art-making are found in the cave paintings in Lascaux, France, which are estimated to be sixteen thousand years old. Human creativity continued to develop and grow over the millennia until something happened in our relatively recent history.

As I mentioned in Chapter 1, more than 90 percent of Americans are left-brain dominant. This means that most of us have either diminished or forgotten our intuitive abilities which are a necessary ingredient for creativity. You may be wondering what happened, how we've gotten so out of balance as a society. In order to understand where our creativity has gone, we'll take a very generalized look at the last few centuries in North America.

Before the arrival of Europeans, the people native to our continent had a creative way of living; they were balanced and naturally in relationship with their environment. They made their own clothing, wove baskets, and crafted beautiful clay pots. They created various kinds of shelter appropriate to the climate in which they lived. The process of making weapons, hunting for food, and growing corn required a great deal of creativity—their survival depended on it. Ceremonies and celebrations were true creative expressions.

Then came the European settlers. The Spanish brought their weaving and wood-carving skills. And they brought the guitar, for which I am very grateful! Creativity was indeed a part of the culture they brought to North America.

Anglo-European pioneers homesteaded the prairie and settled the West, bringing their own customs and expressions of creativity. Along with whistles, drums, and stringed instruments, came literature, storytelling, and poetry. Mere survival on the frontier required a creative way of living. After a hard day of working crops and tending animals, the family would often gather around the woodstove or fireplace. Pulling out their fiddles, banjos, and accordions, they would play tunes and tell stories to create their own entertainment.

Since their arrival in North America as slaves in the 1600s, Africans have made art of many kinds, including quilts, drums, wrought-iron figures, and ceramic vessels. Their plantation-field chanting developed into a unique style of "spiritual" singing that later moved into black churches and beyond, eventually branching out into blues, jazz, and rock and roll. Whether you love it or hate it, you can thank Africans for introducing the banjo to North America!

With this amazing tapestry of creativity that made up our North American culture, things began to change in the mid-1800s. The Industrial Revolution virtually took over our society. Imagine the creativity it took to invent the steam engine, railroads, and machines of mass production. Look at Henry Ford and Thomas Edison: true creativity in action. This was indeed a creative time for some. The trouble was, workers were needed to do very repetitive (noncreative) jobs, operating the machines and working the production lines. This monotonous work allowed the creative muscles of the masses to atrophy. For the first time in human history, creativity was not a requirement for survival.

Another reason that the Industrial Revolution is so significant in the history of creativity is that our current educational system—which tends to minimize creativity—was developed then, and some might say it has changed very little since. Roger Sperry, who did the split-brain research in the 1970s, said that "our educational system, as well as science in general, tends to neglect the nonverbal form of intellect. What it comes down to is that modern [Western] society discriminates against the right hemisphere." Dianne Crampton, corporate consultant and author of *TIGERS Among Us*, puts it this way: "Our educational system was developed in the Industrial Age to turn out people who would fit into hierarchical work environments, that is, who would do what they are told."

In the early 1900s came the introduction of the radio. Instead of playing and listening to live music and telling stories, the family would gather around the radio after dinner and listen to news from around the world and music being played by others. The "greats"—Glenn Miller, the Dorseys, Billie Holiday, to name a few—were the ones who made the music, and gradually we became a society of listeners rather than creators. As you read in the section on the magic of live performance in Chapter 2, there is a big difference between listening passively to a radio and participating in a live music or theater event. With passive listening, we're missing out on the transformative energy flow between performer and audience.

In the 1950s the television entered our living rooms. We gathered around the tube and became not only listeners but watchers, too. Can you say "couch potato"?

Ironically, the overuse of these inventions has caused a glitch in the development of the very human creativity that brought them into existence. I'm not saying that radio and television are inherently bad—there is indeed great value in these technological advances, particularly in the uplifting programming of public radio and public television—but it's interesting to notice how they have stunted our growth in terms of creativity. Much of the time we used to spend telling stories, singing, and quilting (interacting with one another) is now spent passively listening and watching, which tend to drain energy and creativity rather than increase it.

As we left the Industrial Age and moved into the Information Age—the age of briefcases, computers, and mass communication—our schools evolved to turn out armies of analytical thinkers who would fit into the corporate workforce. On the surface, there was nothing wrong with this left-brain emphasis in education because that's who we needed to be at the time. The problem is that the majority of us had forgotten how to use the intuitive and spiritually connected right hemisphere of our brains.

In the 1960s, many young people felt oppressed by the left-brain-dominant society. *Father Knows Best* and *Leave It to Beaver* were not very creative lifestyle models. "There must be a better way," we thought. The good part of a generation—now known as the Cultural Creatives, a term coined by Paul Ray and Sherry Anderson—jumped ship and went searching for a more right-brain existence. Yes, it was an extreme reaction back then, but now we're beginning to integrate some of the ideals of the Cultural Creatives. Moving toward a more balanced way of life, the sixties generation brought forth many activities and concepts—yoga, meditation, massage, spiritual seeking, organic foods, and eco-consciousness—that are becoming mainstream today.

We're moving out of the Information Age now and, according to Daniel Pink, many of the information jobs we've been trained to do can be performed in Asia for less money or done more accurately by computers. The good news, however, is that this mass exodus of analytical jobs is forcing us to get back to developing right-brain qualities that can't be outsourced or computerized. "The future belongs to a very different kind of person with a very different kind of mind—creators and empathizers, pattern recognizers, and meaning makers. These people—artists, inventors, designers, storytellers, caregivers, consolers, big picture thinkers—will now reap society's richest rewards and share its greatest joys," says Pink.

Illustration from *A Whole New Mind*,
Daniel Pink (Penguin, 2005)

Now, at the dawn of the twenty-first century, it's time to bring back the creativity that we've lost along the way. If we are to survive as a species, we must get back, as Einstein said, to honoring the sacred gift of the intuitive mind and putting the rational mind back in its place as servant. Let's put our right minds back in the driver's seat!

INDIVIDUAL CREATIVITY

Now we'll take a look at how creativity changes over the course of an individual's lifetime. You may recall some of the experiences I had that turned me inward and shut me down creatively. Remember the third-grade chorus experience? And the continual reprimands for daydreaming? How about the way I took refuge in analytical hobbies like building model airplanes and trains? Or the time I quit piano lessons because I was so afraid of getting up in front of an audience at the recital? Fortunately I had the opportunity to reclaim a piece of my creativity as a teenager through playing guitar in a band. What is unfortunate is that many of us move well into adulthood without ever reconnecting with our creative selves. If you're like me, and you've allowed negative childhood experiences to compromise your creativity, it's my sincere hope that this book will help you reconnect with your creative self.

ALL children are **artists** the problem is to REMAIN an artist as we **grow up**

—PABLO PICASSO

Austin, Texas, singer/songwriter/artist/teacher Sara Hickman believes that children are naturally creative. Here's what she said in her 2006 *Art of the Song* interview:

I try to share with people—when I'm teaching or speaking with parents—that we don't come into this world this blank slate, and people need to fill us up with information. No, no, no. We come into this world brilliant, and it's the job of the parents and the teachers to get out of the way of these children and help them to express what's inside to come out. I think in Western culture in particular, we dampen that very quickly: "You need to do it this way." "Are you listening to me?" "Why would you do that?" "I cannot believe you talk that way." "Do not treat your sister that way." It's a lot of heavy-handed control. We're ready. When we come into this world we have all the gifts we need.

In his 2008 *Art of the Song* interview, Canadian singer/songwriter Bruce Cockburn told us a story about taking an art class at the age of four. He and his fellow students were painting Christmas cards with watercolors.

I painted a scene. It had a pine tree and a crescent moon, and a cloud up there. The teacher came around and looked at my work and said, "You can't have a cloud above the moon. Clouds can't be higher than the moon." If I'd have been a different kind of person and actually bought that, there would have gone a chunk of my creativity right there. If you have too many occasions like that, it's going to stunt your growth, I think.

Whether it was criticizing for coloring outside the lines or singing a little out of tune, misguided teachers have shut down countless wonderful creative minds and hearts before their time. Fortunately there are many good artist-in-residence programs that help children stay connected with their creativity. One such program is headed up by songwriter and teacher Paul Reisler, whose very successful Kid Pan Alley places professional songwriters in elementary schools to write songs with children. Reflecting on his many Kid Pan Alley residencies across the country, Paul told us that our schools are not teaching children to be creators but rather to be consumers. In his 2006 *Art of the Song* interview, he said:

> The creative act is the most powerful thing in the world. Everything of value in this world is made by people creating something...people having an idea, getting an image in their mind, and then creating it. And yet we're not teaching our kids how to be creative, we're teaching them the opposite.

I think a lot of so-called midlife crises come about as a result of repressed creativity. We get to a point in life when we've played by the rules for so long that we've put the guitar (figuratively speaking) in the closet, or we've never learned to play it in the first place. Eventually something gives and, in a manner of speaking, we explode—sometimes slowly, sometimes quickly. This is a good thing because it gives us the opportunity to change direction and to invite the missing creativity back into our lives. In the cosmic game of hide-and-seek, this is the time when we take the blindfold off and turn back to rediscover our creative selves. In many cases, it's the midlife crisis that gives us the nudge to change direction.

Fortunately we don't have to wait for midlife to rediscover our creativity. As we continue to recognize the importance of creativity in our society, it will become easier for people to remain creative through early life and on into adulthood. As our societal "creativity quotient" increases, it will be more natural for people to be employed in creative work that they love and enjoy. If we are truly doing our creative passion as our work, would we ever want to retire? Well, maybe...to pursue other creative activities. Our society is based on the concept of doing jobs for money not necessarily for passion. So, many of us put off doing what we really love, and when we retire—if we're lucky enough to live that long—then we get to do it. The trouble is that doing a job for the wrong reasons takes a toll and often results in poor health. If you've worked in a left-brain-dominant job for a full career and you're nearing retirement, this could well be your opportunity to dive into the wonderful world of creative exploration.

SPIRITUAL QUEST

Engaging in a creative activity has the potential to bring us closer to God or a higher power. Like long ago, when we would find ourselves captivated in childhood play and time seemed to stand still, when we completely lose ourselves in writing, drawing, playing music, or anything creative, we allow spirit to flow through us. Said another way, putting the ego self aside—as can happen during this timeless state of creative bliss—allows the space for our inner being to shine through.

the quest for **spirituality** is the greatest **mega-trend** of our era... in 1994, the Gallup people asked AMERICANS if they felt the need to experience SPIRITUAL GROWTH ONLY 20 percent said "YES"
in 1999, they asked again—and a surprising 78 percent answered in the AFFIRMATIVE
an **astounding** 58 percentage point GAIN in five years.
—PATRICIA ABURDENE, *Megatrends 2010*

As you'll learn in Chapter 4, the true creative process is a mind, body, spirit experience. The trinity of mind, body, and spirit is referenced in many religions. Holistic healers describe perfect health as a harmonious alignment of mind, body, and spirit. Would it not make sense that when all three are aligned, as they are in the creative process, one could have a spiritual experience?

In *The Well of Creativity*, Michael Toms had this to say after interviewing *Artist's Way* author Julia Cameron about the spiritual nature of creativity: "[She] believes that one of the ways to connect with the greater spirit of the world is through our creativity. No traditional concept of God is necessary to succeed, only a sense that our personal creativity reflects that of the universe, and as we express our artistic impulses we come in touch with a spiritual world of infinite size and power."

Exploring and expressing our creativity is one way of getting to that divine part of ourselves. There are many other ways, such as meditation and prayer, engaging in a physical activity to the point of experiencing the flow, or simply walking in nature and appreciating the natural world around us.

Vivian and I were artists in residence at St. John's Episcopal Cathedral in Albuquerque during 2008 and 2009. Our mission was to explore the relationship between creativity and spirituality with the parishioners. We conducted a series of monthly workshops and found that there are indeed many similarities between creativity and spirituality. The findings are published in the book *A Creative Spirit*, written and edited by Vivian Nesbitt. Here's what the Very Reverend Mark Goodman, dean and rector of the cathedral, had to say about the relationship between creativity and spirituality: "In the story of Creation, we are told that humans were created 'in the image of God.' That phrase means a great many things, but at least one thing it means is that, like God, we are creative beings. The creative urge lies within each one of us and manifests itself in multiple ways. As we explore the creative spirit within us, we learn something about God in whose image we are made."

Theologian Matthew Fox wrote a book called *Creativity: Where the Divine and the Human Meet*. The very title of his book suggests that creativity is intimately connected with divinity. This is how Fox describes the relationship: "We are creators at our very core. Only creating can make us happy, for in creating we tap into the deepest powers of self and universe and the Divine Self. We become co-creators, that is, we create *with* the other forces of society, universe, and the Godself when we commit to creativity."

In *The Zen of Creativity*, John Daido Loori talks about creativity from a Zen Buddhist perspective: "The creative process, like a spiritual journey, is intuitive, non-linear, and experiential. It points us toward our essential nature, which is a reflection of the boundless creativity of the universe. Zen Buddhism, and particularly the Zen arts are a rich source of teachings to help us understand and cultivate our creativity."

It's interesting to notice the similarities between the "flow" experienced during the creative process and during a spiritual (or perhaps religious) experience. Seeking spiritual awareness and creativity are one and the same, because it is the spiritual part of you that is infinitely and naturally creative. So engaging in the creative process has the potential to raise your awareness and connect you to a greater spiritual reality. It's also interesting to note that the process works in both directions—you can access your spiritual self through creativity, *and* you can access your creativity through following a spiritual path. Creativity can be both the means and the end, the path and the destination. At the very least, exploring creativity is an excellent and fun way to deepen your spiritual journey.

Creativity, for most of us, abounds early in life, then something begins to happen that dampens our ability to freely express ourselves. We become conditioned by our left-brain-dominant society. We go through dark periods where the connection to our naturally creative selves becomes obscured by life's demands and concerns. Eventually, if we are among the fortunate, something draws us back to our creative roots. This process can be viewed in the context of a spiritual awakening, the cosmic game of hide-and-seek.

Could it be that our species is facing a midlife crisis of its own? Have we gotten so far away from our indigenous roots that—like a forty-five-year-old—we're beginning to notice that something is missing? Perhaps the current economic crisis, fed by rampant consumerism and greed, and the frustration of our deeply polarized society are providing the much-needed wake-up call, nudging us ever closer to a creative awakening. I believe we are on the verge of a great creative renaissance. Fortunately for us and for our society, a few manage to negotiate their way through life without losing the creativity that was their gift at birth. These are the artists, musicians, writers, and dancers who inspire us on a regular basis, and whose gifts shine as beacons to the rest of us as an example of what's possible. If we follow their lead and the Truth in our own hearts, we will flourish individually and as a society. No one can do it for us. Government can't do it. We must do the work individually and in small groups (you'll learn how in Chapter 5), gradually spreading the creative message until we reach the tipping point.

KEY POINTS

1. Creativity is essentially what defined the beginning of our human existence more than forty thousand years ago. Creativity grew steadily with human evolution until the 1800s with the advent of the Industrial Revolution, when creativity began to wane in the masses. The advent of radio and television hastened the demise of creativity in our society.

2. We're born creative, but in most cases, life's experiences tend to diminish our ability to access creativity.

3. If we've not kept our creativity alive, we may get an opportunity, often in midlife, to turn back to our creative selves.

4. Our society is facing a midlife crisis of its own. It's time to recognize the need and turn back to creativity.

ACTION STEPS

1. Review your family's ancestry. Do you have parents, grandparents, great- or great-great-grandparents who played a musical instrument or had another creative outlet like quilting or storytelling? Write in your creativity journal about how your heritage has influenced your own creativity.

2. In Action Step 1 at the end of Chapter 2, you wrote about a childhood event that might have closed down your creativity. Take that experience and turn it around by making it into an affirmation. For example, remembering my experience of singing in the third-grade chorus, I might create the affirmation: "I have a strong voice, and I always sing on key." Remember affirmations are your Authentic Self calling to you from the future, saying, "You can do it!" Post this affirmation on your mirror, refrigerator, and at your desk so you see it frequently, and repeat it to yourself often throughout the day.

3. Think about where you are with your personal creativity. Have you been fully in touch with your creative self all your life? If you've lost a chunk of your creativity somewhere along the way, do you

think it's time to bring it back? Maybe you've gone through a midlife crisis (or several like me) and you're now rediscovering your creativity. Write about these thoughts in your creativity journal.

4. If you find yourself in a place where you'd like to add more creativity to your life, think about how you'd like to do it and take an action step toward bringing it into your life. For example, if you decide you'd like to explore painting, you might go to the art-supply store and buy some paints and a couple of canvases.

the **creative** process, like a SPIRITUAL JOURNEY, is **intuitive, non-linear**, and **experiential**
—JOHN DAIDO LOORI, *The Zen of Creativity,*

The Three Phases
of Creativity

the dictionary defines creativity as "to make or
bring into **existence** something new"
my definition of the creative process gets a little
more **specific**: to make or bring into existence
something NEW. by generating **ideas** (right
brain); developing, **reorganizing**, and refining
them (left brain); and taking physical **action**

■ As I've mentioned, before my present life as host and pro-
ducer of *Art of the Song: Creativity Radio*, I had a successful career
as a guitar maker. Among the instruments I'd built over the
years were guitars for Steve Earle, Trisha Yearwood, Hank
Williams Jr., the Mavericks, Michael Martin Murphey, and
Tish Hinojosa, to name a few.

I had never thought of making guitars as a truly creative act. After all, it was a very linear process of cutting out

pieces of wood, shaping them, and gluing them together. If one knew the sequence and followed instructions—there are many books that describe the process—then one could build a guitar, right?

At a recent meeting, my mentor Jim Folkman, who was working with me in a leadership training course, asked me to

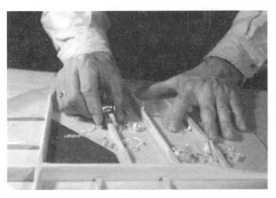

describe the process of building a guitar. I told him about the conversation with the client for whom I was building the instrument, and that to me the interesting part was designing the "perfect" guitar for that person. It was about finding out what the client wanted in terms of sound, feel, and look. Sometimes the client could articulate exactly what he or she was looking for in the ideal guitar, and sometimes I had to ask a lot of questions and use my experience and intuition to design the instrument. I began to realize, as I was describing the process to Jim, that this design phase was indeed a very creative, intuitive process. Once the guitar was designed, it was more a matter of following the steps in a logical sequence. Also integral to the construction phase is the very intuitive process of shaving the braces and tapping the top until it sounds just right—a process that distinguishes handmade instruments from factory-made ones. This involves chiseling away bits of wood from the braces and then holding up the spruce top between two fingers and tapping it with a knuckle, repeating the process until the desired sound is achieved. Jim responded, "You mean it's the spirit and the mind working together?" "Exactly," I said, "and to that you add the body—the working with the hands, the physical skill to bring something new into the world."

For the first time, I truly understood that the creative process is not just the right-brain function that it is commonly thought to be. It is a process that involves three distinct elements—right- and left-brain thinking, combined with the physical act of making. Building a beautiful, great-sounding guitar requires the design, the logical thinking, and the assembly.

This understanding of creativity is borne out through the many *Art of the Song* interviews we've conducted with songwriters, who say that their process involves both the inspiration (receiving the idea) and the crafting of the song (editing). In the past I've thought of the inspiration as the creative part and the crafting as not necessarily creative. In the case of songwriting, the physical part is playing chords on an instrument, singing, and writing down the lyrics.

The creative process is literally an integration of left- and right-brain thinking and some aspect of the body, a holistic combination of the analytical, physical, and intuitive—mind, body, and spirit. I guess I knew this on some level, but relating it to my guitar-making really drove the concept home for me.

THE THREE PHASES OF CREATIVITY

Let's go into depth for each of the three phases of creativity. The following framework will make creativity easy to understand, and when you understand it, it will become easier to access. Put simply, creativity is a three-phase process, consisting of the spirit, the body, and the mind. Said another way, creativity occurs at the intersection of inspiration, action, and analysis. These three phases can happen in any order or, in some cases, simultaneously. Often the creator moves randomly from one phase to another.

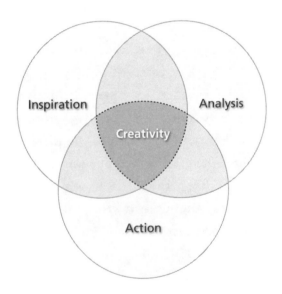

Inspiration + Action + Analysis = **Creativity**

Inspiration (Spirit)

The inspiration phase is the insight, the generation of an original idea. This is the right-brain part of the process. You might wake up in the middle of the night with a solution to a problem you've been facing at work. You might be driving and suddenly hear a melody in your head for a new song. Or you might overhear some gossip in the booth next you at a coffee shop and decide to write a short story about it. This is the mysterious part of the creative process, often referred to as courting the muse. You can't have creativity without inspiration. I'll go into greater detail here because this is the least-understood phase of the creative process.

Although you cannot control when inspiration will strike, there are many things you can do to create the right conditions. Having a regular practice of doing your creative activity every day at the same time helps. Having a special place in your home or office where you do your creative work/play will help, too. Creating a ritual—lighting a candle or incense, reading an inspirational quote—that you repeat every time you sit down to create can help invoke the muse. I find that doing a short meditation helps to get me in a receptive state. Some of the songwriters we've interviewed on *Art of the Song* are very disciplined about their process, and some simply wait for inspiration to come and then they sit down to write.

In her 2007 *Art of the Song* interview, singer/songwriter Susan Werner told us about a few little tricks she does to court the muse:

> Everybody has a reason to freak out about the stuff not happening on your own timetable. But [the muse] really does show up, almost when you're not looking, doing the dishes and the idea shows up. I think being engaged with your hands is important. In my office I keep darts, juggling balls. I think knitting, if you're interested in the needle arts. These things do occupy your hands, and I think that sets your brain free. Doing the dishes, folding the laundry is a place where a lot of good ideas come to me. It's just putting the stupid socks together. Somehow your hands are occupied so your brain is free.

Free-writing—writing with pen and paper for a set period of time, keeping the pen moving no matter what comes out—is a way to tap into the intuitive side of the brain, to generate new ideas. This is an example of one of my recent morning free-writes (edited for punctuation only). It came after I'd been wondering about the creative muse as I went to sleep the night before. I share it here to demonstrate the form (or, rather, lack thereof) of the free-write as well as to show the kind of content that can be generated by tapping into the intuition.

Meditation to prepare for creativity; meditation to court the muse. It's all about quieting the mind, setting the ego aside so that we can connect with our higher selves, our muse. What is the muse? Is it something outside ourselves? Is it something far away? No. The muse—as it is often referred to by artists and writers—is simply the higher expanded part of ourselves that is who we really are. We are spiritual beings on an earthly journey here and now. When we stop our activity and quiet the mind we can relax into our expanded being, who we really are. This is the way to access our creativity. This is the way to manifest in the world. This is the way to find our life purpose and make a meaningful contribution to the world. I love being in the creative flow.

Free-writing is an integral part of the 20-20 Practice, which you'll learn about in Chapter 5.

Some say inspiration comes from within, and some say it comes from outside ourselves. Songwriter Mary Gauthier talks about a lightning bolt of inspiration coming from the Creator, and that she is but a lightning rod attracting the lightning, the song idea. Nashville writer Beth Nielsen Chapman claims that songs are somewhere "out there" already written, and that she as a writer must tune in to them and bring them into form. Country songwriter Dave Gibson says that the songs are in his guitar and his job is to pull them out. When I delivered the custom guitar I made for him, Dave played it for a while and then said, "There are a lot of good songs in this guitar!"

However you choose to envision inspiration, when it comes, it's important to let it flow and keep the left-brain critic out of the way. The best way to receive inspiration is to cultivate a state of awareness at all times. Keep your creative antennae up by always being aware of what your senses—sight, sound, smell, taste, and touch—*and* your emotions are telling you. And, be ready to write it down or speak/sing it into a recorder (action).

Action (Body)

Taking physical action is essential to the process of bringing something new into existence. This usually involves some kind of learned skill—pen to paper, brush to canvas, chisel to wood, or finger to fretboard. Taking action—whether it be writing or typing, playing a musical instrument, speaking, singing, acting, or dancing—concretizes the inspiration and brings it into the physical plane. Having a great idea is wonderful, but it won't do anybody any good unless it is brought into physical form. Many songwriters keep a notebook or a pocket recorder with them at all times so they never lose a potential song idea. As Guy Clark told us in his *Art of the Song* interview, he wrote the chorus lyrics to "L.A. Freeway" in the back of a cab on a napkin with his wife's eyeliner pencil.

Action can also be used to jump-start the inspiration phase of creativity. Just sitting down to do your creative work/play can open you up to inspiration. Berklee College of Music professor Pat Pattison says that the degree of writers block is directly proportional to the distance from your butt to the chair. And, remember what Susan Werner said about keeping the hands occupied in order to set the mind free. This illustrates the essential interaction between body and spirit.

Analysis (Mind)

Analysis is the left-brain part of the creative process. This is where you develop, reorganize, and refine the idea—the editing process in the case of writing or songwriting. It's the testing and researching part of scientific discovery. Learning theory and how to read music is the left-brain part of becoming a great musician.

In nearly every form of creative expression all three phases are used, but not necessarily at the time of the creative event. I've heard of a few instances when a songwriter was literally *given* a song and it came through from inspiration to action in one fell swoop without the analysis phase being present, almost like channeling. In these cases, however, the left-brain work of learning songwriting technique and language *was* still part of the equation—it had been done prior to the creative event. Another example of what I call spontaneous creativity occurs when a jazz or blues player knows his instrument and the framework of the song so well that he can improvise a solo purely from right-brain inspiration, "without thinking." He did the left-brain work of practicing his scales and learning the song ahead of time.

THREE PHASES IN A SONG

Let's look at songwriting to illustrate how the three phases of creativity interact with one another. As you've learned above, inspiration for a song can come in many ways. I may be driving in the car, with scenery flying by, and an idea comes to me, or I may overhear someone say something in a restaurant and think to myself, "There's an idea for a song." Usually some kind of sensory input—be it sight, sound, smell, taste, touch, or emotion—will trigger the inspiration.

When I wrote "New Mexico Moon," I was living in the East and it had been a long hot summer. Then one of those clear, low-humidity days seemed to come out of nowhere—big blue sky with high cirrus clouds. I thought about how the weather was like that most of the time in northern New Mexico, having lived there during the 1970s. I began to muse about how I really wanted to move back. My second wife, Tory, and I had been having conversations about how difficult it was to make a living in the rural community of Taos, and she didn't think we should make a move unless we had a foolproof financial plan in place. I really missed the West.

So the clear blue sky, the dry weather, and my sense of longing for the West were the initial inspiration. I began writing (action) words and phrases that evoked images of New Mexico: western sky, wispy clouds, pink adobe, waltz around the dance floor.

Often, at this stage, I'll do a free-write for ten minutes or so to get down as many words and images as I can on the subject. I just keep the pen moving or fingers typing and let the ideas flow. This is not the time for analysis. I try to keep the critical left-brain voice silent (which isn't always easy). Then I'll circle or highlight words and phrases that jump out, and write them on another page. This gives me more raw material to work with. While engaging in this process of playing with words and phrases (analysis), often another idea (inspiration) will come to me. I like working on a computer because the ability to cut and paste and move things around stimulates my creativity and makes the editing easier.

After moving words around and looking for a rhyme (analysis) the first two lines came together:

Cool western sky blew in last night
High wispy clouds and the air was right

It's a very fluid process. I picked up the guitar and started playing with some chords and a waltz rhythm (action). I started saying the words over the chords and poked around for a melody. I repeated the three phases of creativity—inspiration, analysis, action—over and over in various combinations until I had the first verse:

Cool western sky blew in last night
High wispy clouds and the air was right
Made me remember my heart's desire
The sweet smell of sagebrush and sunsets of fire

The idea for the chorus came from the conversation I'd had with Tory about finances and figuring out how to make a living in New Mexico. After working the three phases for a while, this is what emerged:

I don't need to be rich, don't want to be poor
I just wanna sing while you dance 'cross the floor
Want a warm cozy room to write down a tune
With a view of the mountains and New Mexico moon

At some point during the writing process—as often happens—the song takes on a life of its own. This is when I try to get out of the way and see what the song wants. It's no longer *me* writing the song, but the song writing itself through me. I'll ask myself not "What do *I* want to say here" but rather "What does the *song* want to say here." My subconscious mind works on the song while I'm doing other things. I may get an idea out of the blue, or wake up in the middle of the night with the perfect word or phrase. This is when I really know the creative process is working.

Now that I had the framework, I began working with different images and phrases to tell the story of my desire to move back to New Mexico. It became like a puzzle looking for the right words and rhymes to fill in for each verse.

Once the rough song was in place, it became a matter of bringing in the editor part of my brain (analysis) and fine-tuning and polishing the song. You'll notice that I made slight changes in the choruses as the song progresses. Here are the completed lyrics.

Cool western sky blew in last night
High wispy clouds and the air was right
Made me remember my heart's desire
The sweet smell of sagebrush and sunsets of fire

There's a small pink adobe that's easy to keep
A garden to grow and a harvest to reap
A home for my family to love and to learn
Some things you save and some things you burn

(Chorus)
I don't need to be rich, don't want to be poor
I just wanna sing while you dance 'cross the floor
Want a warm cozy room to write down a tune
With a view of the mountains and New Mexico moon

Thunderstorm's rolling out over the plains
I can feel the sun shining up through the rain

When the storm clouds scatter and darkness falls
Full moon lights the night and coyote calls

(Chorus)
I don't need to be rich, don't want to be poor
I wanna play my guitar while you waltz 'cross the floor
Want a warm cozy room to write down a tune
With a view of the mountains and New Mexico moon

Life is a journey, a mystery
The trail we've traveled is history
The future is a flower yet to unfold
But this present moment is the gift to behold

Cool western sky blew in last night
High wispy clouds and the air is right
Though I live in the East and I'm not leaving soon
Deep in my heart is the New Mexico moon

(Chorus)
I don't need to be rich, and I'll never be poor
'Cause I play this guitar while you dance 'cross the floor
I've got a warm cozy room where I wrote down this tune
I can feel it in my heart, the New Mexico moon

It's interesting to note that the process of writing this song actually brought about a personal transformation for me (as described in the final verses and chorus). The process helped me work through a difficult period in my life—as manifested by my desire to go back to New Mexico—and brought me to a place of acceptance through the realization that I could be happy just about anywhere if I could live in the present moment and carry the feeling of the "New Mexico Moon" with me in my heart. Writing "New Mexico Moon" brought me out of a depression to a place of actually feeling good about my life again. I eventually did move back to New Mexico, though it was several years later.

If you'd like to hear the finished tune, there is a free audio download of "New Mexico Moon" at:

2020CreativitySolution.com

The harmony vocal is sung by my friend and a former New Mexico resident Tish Hinojosa.

KEY POINTS

1. Creativity is a three-phase process that occurs at the intersection of inspiration, action, and analysis. The phases can occur in any order or simultaneously.

2. Inspiration is the generation of a new idea, a right-brain process.

3. Action involves taking the idea and bringing it into physical form.

4. Analysis is the left-brain phase of editing, refining, and changing the original idea.

ACTION STEPS

1. Think of the two phases of creativity that involve thinking: inspiration and analysis. Which phase resonates with you? Which are you good at? Are you well-balanced in your use of the right and left brains, or is there one that could use some development? Write about this in your creativity journal.

2. Think about inspiration as it pertains to your chosen form of creative expression. If you don't have a chosen creative activity, think about something you've always dreamed of creating, or just think about living every day as creatively as possible. Create a vision of where inspiration comes from for you. Remember the stories from Susan Werner, Mary Gauthier, Beth Nielsen Chapman, and Dave Gibson? Your vision may be connected to your spiritual or religious beliefs, or not. Whatever works for you, it's helpful to create a visual image. In your creativity journal, draw a picture or describe your vision of where inspiration comes from.

3. Make up your own ritual for courting the muse or creating the right conditions for inspiration. Fix up a place in your home or office to be your creative space. Think about setting aside a certain time each day to create. You don't have to commit to it yet; just think about what would be a good time for you. When during the day do you feel most creative?

5

The 20-20 Practice

we're tapping into SOMETHING, some part
of ourselves, our **soul** and our **mind**, that we're
not aware of in our daily life...
and I think it's a way of GETTING at a
truth when you can't get at it any other way
—MEG HUTCHINSON
singer/songwriter, interview for *Art of the Song*

FROM INTENTION TO CREATIVITY

■ *Intend* that you will access your natural creativity. *Believe* that you can. *Trust* that you have something unique and beautiful to offer the world. *Do it.*

It all starts with intention. Nothing happens without intention. It's the *deciding* to be creative. It's also about giving yourself *permission* to create. You see, many of us have been taught that creative expression is frivolous, childish, or negative in some other way. So we need to be able to say to ourselves, "It's okay to be creative," or "Creativity is my birthright, and I *will* express my creative voice."

Intention sets the foundation, the place from which to create. It begins the thought process. It acts like a magnet that attracts ideas. If creativity is the process of turning a thought or an idea into reality, then intention is what focuses the thought process in the desired direction. Intention can be applied on an event-by-event basis—"I am going to write a song or poem, paint a painting"—or it can be an ongoing state: "I am a creator." Intention is saying to the universe, "I am ready...I am open!"

Intend to be a creative. Believe that you are naturally creative. Trust yourself. Take action to create a life that supports your intention, and tap into the infinite power of creativity!

THE 20-20 PRACTICE

The 20-20 Practice is a simple four-part process you can use to facilitate your journey home to your Authentic Self and thus awaken your natural creativity. I call it the 20-20 Practice because all it takes is twenty minutes before you sleep at night and twenty minutes when you wake up in the morning. "20-20" also represents the clarity of vision you'll have when you're in harmony with your Authentic Self. This is not a "creative practice" in and of itself; it is a method to clear the decks and prepare the way to more effectively do your creative work/play, whatever that might be. If you already have a regular creative practice, this process will be like a fine cup of espresso to further stimulate your creativity. If you don't have a specific creative practice, the 20-20 will open you to a new level of creativity in everything you do.

Over the years, I've studied a number of wisdom traditions and participated in several personal-development paths. This practice is a synthesis of what I've found to be the most effective ways to access creativity. The elements of the practice and their sequence have been tested and tweaked by me and a group of volunteers from across the country. Nearly everyone who has diligently applied the practice has reported positive results.

What this process will do, if practiced regularly, is allow your Authentic (creative) Self to shine through in everything you do. It's about correcting your course every day, which ultimately results in living a life of integrity and of unity with your Authentic Self. The practice is easy to do but does require a measure of discipline and consistency to achieve results. Unlike many personal-development practices that begin in the morning, the 20-20 Practice begins in the evening, right before you go to sleep. Think of the practice as bookends to make your sleep time more productive.

There is no right or wrong way to do the practice. These are only suggestions. The basic concepts have worked for thousands of people all over the world. I suggest that you start doing the 20-20 as written, then feel free to change and mold the steps to fit your style of living. The practice can be done "loosely but with firm commitments," as personal-development mentor Jesse White suggests. I invite you to commit to doing the practice for three weeks, then decide for yourself if you want to continue.

Part 1: Clear Your Plate

This part of the 20-20 Practice is designed to clear the mind and release any anxiety you may have accumulated during the day. It's also about taking full responsibility for everything that shows up in your life.

Completely ready to retire, you may do these exercises sitting up in bed (my preference), in a comfortable chair, or at your desk.

1. Close your eyes and review your day starting with the most recent events going back through the day in reverse. After you've gotten back to the beginning of the day, ask yourself the following questions.

2. "What are the things that happened today for which I have gratitude?" Think of things that you accomplished today, things that you are proud of, and things that others did that you admire.

Rejoice! Make a list in your notebook of three to five "gratitudes" that stand out.

3. "What things would I have done differently if I had a second chance?" Write these down.

4. "Is there anyone I should apologize to?" This may be someone from today or from the past. If there is someone, close your eyes, picture that person in your mind, and imagine yourself saying, "I'm sorry, _____." Do this three times per person, then let the image fade.

5. "Is there anyone I need to forgive?" This also may be someone from today or from the past. If there is someone, see that person in your mind and say to yourself, "I forgive you, _____." Do this three times per person, then *forgive yourself* for your part in the event. Remember you are responsible for your stories. Finally, ask the universe for forgiveness, saying silently, "Please forgive me," three times.

6. Make a list of the three most important things you want to get done tomorrow.

Part I should take about ten to fifteen minutes. You should now feel very relaxed and positive.

Part 2: Task the Subconscious Mind

Now lie down in bed ready for sleep. With your eyes closed:

7. Think of the people in your life you would like to send love to—family, friends, acquaintances, or business associates. These could be people you really do love, or people you feel you may not love enough. Picture one person at a time and silently say to yourself, "I love you, _____" (three times per person). Finish by loving *yourself*. If saying, "I love you," feels uncomfortable or too personal, try saying, "With a beam of love I touch your heart, _____." I learned this technique from artist and spiritual teacher, Herman Rednick.

8. Now think of a few people, things, or situations in your life for which you have *major* gratitude. Really *feel* that gratitude. Thank the universe for your wonderful life. Rejoice!

9. Visualize a particular creative project you are working on, or perhaps a problem for which you would like a creative solution. Imagine the project or problem in your mind's eye. This is

not the time for analysis. Rather, let the thoughts float by and cultivate a state of wondering. Ask yourself, "I wonder what would be a good solution for this problem or situation?" If you don't have something specific, you may ask, "How might I best express my creativity in the coming days?"

10. With these images and questions, allow yourself to drift off to sleep. You may want to silently repeat the following mantra: *"I am a divine creative being full of passion and grace."* Or simply: *"I am a divine creative being."*

Part 2 shouldn't take more than five minutes. Keep your notebook and pen on your bedside table in case you wake up in the night with an inspiration. Be sure to write your middle-of-the-night insights down because you probably won't remember them in the morning.

Many times during the writing of this book I was unsure about what to say in a certain part of a chapter. So just before sleep, I would ask, "How might I elaborate on this topic? What story could I tell that would illustrate this concept?" Often I would wake up with the perfect solution. For a more detailed discussion of how this part of the practice works, I recommend a book called *Sleep Thinking*, by Eric Maisel (available as a downloadable eBook at 2020CreativitySolution. com).

Part 3: Let It Flow

Immediately upon waking, pick up your notebook and begin writing. Write for five minutes without stopping. Write whatever comes, without thinking or censoring. It doesn't matter if it makes sense or not. The purpose is simply to flow and empty your thoughts onto the paper. This will clear your mind, make it easier to meditate, and free you to be more creative during the day. You might want to use a kitchen timer so you don't have to keep checking the time.

Part 4: Quiet the Mind

Meditate for fifteen minutes or more—whatever is comfortable for you. Meditation is very personal, and you may already have a meditation practice that works for you. There are no hard and fast rules, but here are some suggestions:

Try sitting upright in a comfortable chair, closing your eyes, and breathing slowly and rhythmically. Breathe in for the count of seven and out for the count of seven. Breathe from the diaphragm (the stomach goes in and out, and the chest remains stationary). Start by remembering something you are grateful for. Whatever comes to mind, it could be something from last night's gratitude list or something totally different. The idea is to get in a positive frame of mind. Gratitude tends to help with relaxation and to get fear and the ego out of the way. Now focus your attention on your breath: in and out, in and out. Focusing on the breath brings you into the present moment (the domain of the right brain) and helps to quiet the left brain that lives in the past and future. You may want to silently repeat a mantra like, *"I am a divine creative being. I am a divine creative being."*

The point of meditation is to quiet the analytical mind and open yourself to the right-brain part of yourself that knows no boundaries. Simply allow yourself to expand into your divine infinite being. Whenever a thought enters your mind, just let it float by and refocus on your breath. In - 2 - 3 - 4 - 5 - 6 - 7. Out - 2 - 3 - 4 - 5 - 6 - 7. Breathing slowly and rhythmically helps to quiet the mind. You can visualize this by thinking of your mind as a pond, on which the wind is causing choppy waves and stirring up silt. You can't see to the bottom. As you quiet the left brain and breathe rhythmically, the wind dies down and the water calms. The waves disappear and the silt settles. You can now see clearly to the bottom of the pond (your infinite creative self).

If you're an experienced meditator you may want to go for longer than fifteen minutes. Have your notebook at hand and be ready to write down insights and observations as they occur to you. Finish your meditation by holding a clear intention of expressing your creativity in the world today.

If you have difficulty with meditation, here are a couple of resources: Eric Maisel's *Ten Zen Seconds*, and an audio program called the Holosync® Solution, which induces the brainwave patterns of deep meditation automatically. For information on both, please visit 2020CreativitySolution. com.

. . . .

Once again, I recommend doing the 20-20 Practice every night and morning for at least three weeks. Consistency is important. As you get into doing the practice, I suggest that you write down your thoughts in a notebook or journal. Are you noticing any change in your overall level of creativity? Has your creative work/play been more productive? How do you feel mentally, physically? Are you a better problem solver at work? What changes are you noticing in other areas of your life? If you notice positive results, I invite you to incorporate the 20-20 Practice into your daily routine.

Here are a few words from songwriter Beth DeSombre about how she has fit the practice into her life:

The practice has become so integrated into my life that I can't possibly imagine stopping it...It fits really nicely into my schedule—at night, it replaces the approximately twenty minutes I used to spend reading before bed, and in the morning it replaces the time I used to spend listening to the news. Eventually both the reading and the news-listening are likely to be things I want to have in my life, but as bookends to sleep they're not ideal—this practice does a much better job of sending me off to sleep and getting me started in the day.

THE ELEMENTS OF THE 20-20 PRACTICE

Now that you know the steps of the 20-20 Practice, I'd like to further discuss the elements that make up the practice, why they're included, and how to get the most out of the practice.

The right brain thinks in pictures, so visualizing the events of your day, things you would do differently, those to whom you want to apologize and forgive, and especially those you love, is an extremely powerful way of making real and positive changes in your life.

Evening Practice

1. Daily Review
Reviewing the day in detail is an effective way of becoming more conscious of our actions. When we consciously review the events of the day, we bring our actions to a higher level of awareness. As we do this over time, our actions become more focused and intentional.

2. Gratitude
Gratitude opens us up to our natural creativity. According to physician and author Deepak Chopra, "When you focus on gratitude, your ego gets out of the way and you experience your true Self. You let go of fear and limiting beliefs and feel connected to the divine flow of the universe." This divine flow of the universe is the essence of creativity.

3. Evaluation
Asking ourselves what we would have done differently at the end of each day gives us the opportunity to fine-tune our actions. As we become more aware of the things we wish we had done differently, when similar situations arise in the future, we will tend to act more in accordance with our inner Truth. Over time this has the effect of bringing us more into alignment with our Authentic Selves, and each evening we will notice that there are fewer things that we would want to change.

4. Apology
Silently saying "I'm sorry" to someone we might have offended is another way of raising our actions to a higher level of awareness. We may or may not choose to actually apologize to the person, but simply going through the mental and emotional process of apologizing will make us more conscious during our days and less likely to create situations which require apology. This moves us toward living a life of integrity with our Authentic Selves. Over time there will be fewer needs for apology.

5. Forgiveness
Forgiveness is a way of accepting full responsibility for our state of mind and heart. We can look at it from three different perspectives: forgiving others, forgiving ourselves, and asking the universe for forgiveness.

   Forgiveness is an important part of the clearing process

which allows us to connect with the infinite creative flow of the universe. Holding anger or resentment in our hearts hides us from our Authentic Selves, and thus blocks the flow of creativity. Forgiveness is the agent that can dissolve these blocks. Silently forgiving, as we do in the evening practice, is very helpful for minor day-to-day issues, but occasionally we may need to deal with a major resentment.

This is my formula for forgiving another *and* myself: I first identify the *story* I told myself about the event (that is, the meaning I attached to it), and I remind myself that I'm the one who made up the story. I try to depersonalize the actual *event* as much as possible: "*That* is something that happened, and *this* is the story I told myself about it." I try to understand that we both played a part in a situation I needed to experience in order to learn something important to my personal growth. In other words, I ask myself, "What's the silver lining? What is the lesson to be learned here?" Forgiving both the other person and myself removes blame from both sides of the equation. If there is no blame, there is no one who is wrong, no judgment. Remember, judgment is a left-brain function, and if we're locked up in the left brain, we're closed off from inspiration. I also try to remember that no matter how traumatic an event may have been, it was part of putting the "blindfold" on in the cosmic game of hide-and-seek (to use my analogy from Chapter 2). Remember, we first need to be hidden from the Truth in order to find our way back home.

And finally, asking for forgiveness from the universe—saying, "Please forgive me"—is an act of humility that puts us in a receptive state.

6. Planning

Planning certain elements of our day the night before has the effect not only of making us more effective during the day but also of allowing the subconscious mind to work on them during sleep.

7. Love

Love is the most powerful way to dissolve blocks and transform our limiting beliefs. Here's a quote from my spiritual teacher Herman Rednick: "I remove blocks through love. For love is the divine agent that burns away all karma and opens the door to the Temple."

8. More Gratitude

You can never have too much gratitude! It puts you in harmony with your Authentic Self.

9. Sleep Thinking

Visualizing a project you are working on and tasking the subconscious mind are powerful ways of generating creative solutions while you sleep. We often think of sleep as wasted time in terms of productivity. Why not be productive twenty-four hours a day?

10. Mantra

In Eastern wisdom traditions, a mantra—a word or phrase silently and continually repeated—is often used as an aid to meditation and a means for spiritual centering during the day. It helps to focus the mind and reduce left-brain "chatter." I find it very helpful to use a mantra when falling asleep at night.

Morning Practice

1. Free-writing

Here's what author Allegra Huston offered to someone in the 20-20 Community who was concerned about how she was doing the free-writing:

> You're doing the free-writing perfectly. In fact, as long as you do it at all, you're doing it perfectly. The only way to do it wrong is not to write. There's nothing you're "supposed" to write, nothing that's "supposed" to come up. Perhaps it will be interesting: dreams, ideas, intentions, emotions. Perhaps it will be a struggle and all you'll write is blah blah blah, this is boring, when will this be over. That's OK too. Some people use the analogy of flushing the pipes in the morning, so the blah blah blah works fine for that! But as you've seen, when you write aimlessly, without any particular intention, suggestive phrases

and ideas just pop up, and now you've got something real to take further.

2. Meditation
I went into detail about meditation in the previous section. As an alternative to sitting meditation you might consider doing a yoga practice during this time.

. . . .

If your results with the 20-20 Practice are not all rosy and positive, fear not. This is deep work and may stir up some issues for you. This is normal. In order to reveal your Authentic Self, it's necessary to work through blocks and transform limiting beliefs. I encourage you to do the 20-20 Practice with resolve even if it seems difficult at times. The payoff will be well worth the investment in terms of happiness, fulfillment, and enjoyment of a creative life.

It's very helpful to do the 20-20 Practice with the support of a partner or group. Doing the practice with a group provides inspiration, opportunities for discussion, and accountability. Here's what Karen Szklany Gault had to say about doing the 20-20 with a group:

I was just thinking of the whole group energy dynamic...I think that so many people out there in support of one another's creative energy is powerful medicine. This divine energy just lovingly pulls from each of us our best selves. It would be hard for the most repressed creativity not to manifest itself in a person who keeps up with the Practice.

Support is available through our website:

2020CreativitySolution.com

You'll find information about the 20-20 JumpStart, online community, teleconferences, and other support materials. Vivian and I also offer personal coaching to a limited number of clients.

I'd love to know how the practice is working in your life. Please send your thoughts to me at john@artofthesong.com.

YOUR CREATIVE WORK/PLAY

After completing the morning portion of the 20-20 Practice, I suggest allocating a chunk of time to do your creative work/play—writing, music, making art, or whatever it may be. Perhaps you have to get your kids off to school or go to work yourself, or for some reason find that scheduling a block of time in the morning is difficult. You might want to try setting your alarm sixty to ninety minutes earlier. That's how I wrote this book! If you shorten your sleep time and replace it with a regular meditation and creativity practice, your body, mind, and soul will be nourished as if you had the extra sleep.

If you typically do your creative work/play at a time of day other than morning, you may want to do a shortened version of the morning practice as a starting ritual to put yourself in a creative frame of mind. If you don't have a specific creative activity, no problem. The goal of all of this is to reveal your Authentic Self so that you will be naturally creative in everything you do—to live every day as a work of art. Make a conscious choice to use your intuition more and your analytical mind less.

LOVE more...**think** less!

BENEFITS OF THE 20-20 PRACTICE

As I discussed in Chapter I, there are many benefits to expressing creativity, and many of them are by-products of accessing our Authentic Selves. The 20-20 Practice is a proven method to access the Authentic Self and clear the way for creativity. In addition to more creativity, people who have committed to doing the 20-20 Practice on a regular basis report increased levels of honesty and self-esteem, and a sense of happiness and well-being. Here are some of their thoughts.

Creativity

The 20-20 Practice has provided me with tools to live the Creativity of my life. In other words given me hope and inspiration and perhaps courage, that this is possible for me.—Sally, Albuquerque, NM

It has helped me to see patterns and issues in my life that block my creativity. Leads me to realize how much my creative energy means to me, and how bottlenecked it gets by everyday pressures.—Jean, Taos, NM

I am clear that I am a divine and creative being having a human experience!—Cathy, Bedford, NH

Honesty

One of the things that makes this practice work for me is that it forces me to be honest with myself. I actually had to "think and feel" when doing the practice, which got me to communicate with myself about things I was not otherwise letting myself think about.—Beth, Wellesley, MA

Self-esteem

I feel vibrantly alive, and see my self-esteem rising. After teaching personal development for 22 years, I'm realizing how I've allowed [others] to interfere and negate my success, out of fear of my strength and clarity. The 20-20 shows me how to cultivate support and love for who I am, serve others with clear strength, and deflect negative or unhealthy energy.—Jesse, Durham, NC

Happiness and Well-being

Before I started this practice I had lost my job of 20 plus years which I totally, totally loved, still feeling the pain of divorce (divorced 3 years ago), had a relationship break up after one and a half years, my parents both are in very poor health, and I was going through some health issues. So I was not in a good place to say the least.

After just a week or so of the 20-20 I realized that I had a so much to be grateful for, the nightly exercise confirmed this, the morning meditation cleared my head of negative thoughts and I began to see the world in a much more positive light. I found myself being present to the moment and taking that moment in for all it was worth. Walking from A to B used to be go go go, now I see the people, nature, and I "feel" the moment and I find myself with a smile on my face.

I feel at peace with myself, very few negative thoughts enter my mind, and when one tries to enter it's easy to dismiss it. I feel much more spiritual, I do believe that there is a higher power. I always felt this, but now it is so much more a part of my thinking. I will continue the 20-20.

The 20-20 really has changed my life and the way I see things. I can only say thanks, but the gratitude runs much deeper than any word can say.
—Brian, Boston, MA

The Practice has given me such a sense of well-being...it has returned me to writing every day, so I am satisfied that I am more honest and thinking more creatively in general.—David, Sonoma, CA

THE SHORT LIST

Here is a step-by-step recap of the 20-20 Practice. A free download of this and a special daily guide are available at 2020CreativitySolution.com.

Evening

Sitting up with pen and paper:
1. Daily review (in reverse)
2. Gratitude list
3. What I would change
4. Apology
5. Forgiveness
6. List of three for tomorrow

Lying down with eyes closed:
7. Send love
8. Feel the gratitude
9. Visualize and wonder about a creative project
10. Sleep (*I am a divine creative being*)

Morning

1. Free-write for five minutes
2. Meditate for fifteen minutes; intend to be creative today

KEY POINTS

1. Intention ⇨ Belief ⇨ Trust ⇨ Action. Intend that you will access your natural creativity. Believe that you can. Trust that you have something unique to offer the world. Do it.

2. The 20-20 Practice is made up of four parts, two in the evening and two in the morning, designed to help you integrate with your Authentic Self.

3. Aside from the many intrinsic benefits of bringing yourself into alignment with your Authentic Self, doing so will give you direct access to your natural creativity.

ACTION STEPS

1. Commit to doing the 20-20 Practice for twenty-one days. Begin tonight.

2. Chronicle your journey in your creativity journal.

3. Check out the resources at 2020CreativitySolution.com.

6

Tips to Jump-start
Your Creativity

I BELIEVE in napping
I sleep on the floor in my office
I'll just **lie** down for twenty minutes
just lie down
just SLEEP for a few minutes
and then you get your **brain** back.
—SUSAN WERNER, singer/songwriter,
interview for *Art of the Song*

■ To COMPLEMENT the daily 20-20 Practice, here are some additional ways to tap into your natural creativity.

TAKE A WALK

Going for a brisk walk, whatever time of day, gets the creative juices flowing. Similar to the way sleep thinking works, if you start out with an idea or a question in mind, once you get into the rhythm of walking, you just might be surprised at the insights that pop into your consciousness. The constant moving forward into new scenery stimulates the creative mind.

EXPERIENCE NATURE

Spending time in a natural environment can have a stimulating effect on creativity as well. Think about how our ancestors were naturally creative, and the more we humans became "civilized" (removed from nature), the more our natural creativity faded into the background. Getting back to nature can put us in touch with the creative part of ourselves. I particularly like hiking in the mountains and spending time sitting next to a stream or waterfall. If you live in a city, visit a park or botanical garden, and plan to get out to the country once in a while.

TAKE A SHOWER

This is my personal favorite. Some of my best ideas for songs and business solutions have come to me in the shower. Something about the steady sound and feel of water puts me in a trance and gets my imagination flowing. I read a story about a major hi-tech firm that lost a key idea-generating employee because the company's executives refused to install a shower for him. He moved to another workplace that had a shower, and his warm-water-inspired ideas generated millions of dollars for the new company.

OUT OF THE SILENCE

I find that a constant input of sound from music, TV, and other sources tends to put a damper on inspiration. How can one's mind be open to new ideas when it's being fed a constant stream of other people's ideas and sounds? For me inspiration comes out of the silence. Silence is the fertile ground upon which the seeds of inspiration grow into creative ideas. Out of the silence creativity is born. Even though I'm in the radio business, I rarely have the sound turned on in the car.

Seemingly contradictory to the silence theory, I find it quite stimulating to write in a café or restaurant. I'm usually able to shut out the noise and focus on my own work. The combination of sounds is almost like white noise, which has a hypnotic effect. The energy of people talking and inspiring one another seems to have a positive effect as well.

PICK UP A CREATIVE HOBBY

Learn to play guitar, harmonica, or piano. It's never too late to pick up a musical instrument. Native-style flute is easy to learn and most of the notes sound good together.

Take a process-painting class. Process painting is a fun and effective method to access your subconscious mind through painting—even if you don't know how to paint. The folks at the Painting Experience in the San Francisco Bay Area have been teaching process painting for decades. Here's what they have to say: "The goal is free expression, with the emphasis on the creative process rather than on technique or expertise. [Process painting] is an opportunity to embark on the greatest of all human journeys—embracing your own path and confidently following it."

Try quilting or take a pottery or jewelry-making class. Creative writing is another place to start—we all know how to write! It doesn't matter what you choose, anything you're drawn to will do. *Engaging in a creative activity will stimulate more creativity in all aspects of your life.*

LIMIT PASSIVE ENTERTAINMENT

You read in Chapter 3 about how radio and television have affected us as a society, turning us into passive "consumers" of entertainment. I'm not suggesting that you "Blow up your TV..." as in the John Prine song, but I am suggesting, first of all, be aware of when you're engaging in passive entertainment, and, second, limit yourself to an hour or two per day. You might even try going for a whole day a few times a week without watching any TV. I also suggest being very selective about what you watch. Educational is good; twenty-four-hour news channels, well, not such a good idea. Remember what I said about people watching/listening to news programming that supports their limiting beliefs (this goes both ways, liberal or conservative). Author and creativity expert Suzanne Falter-Barns says, "The creative part of yourself is sensitive, easily upset by the negative stream that passes through the news desks of our nation. Therefore, limit or completely turn off the news. Once you wean yourself of it, you'll find that you really don't care what the headlines are." Good drama and movies definitely have a place when you just want to relax and be entertained for an hour or two.

PARTICIPATE IN ACTIVE ENTERTAINMENT

Engage more in *active* entertainment such as going to a play, a reading, or a live concert. Go out dancing to a live band or to a DJ who spins original music. Visit an art gallery or a museum this week. There is something about the interaction between artist and audience that stimulates creativity. Remember the energy flow of live concerts I talked about in Chapter 2?

There is a phenomenon that has been growing across the country in the last couple of decades called "house concerts." These are small concerts (usually twenty to fifty in the audience) held in a living room without a PA system—acoustic music in an intimate setting. Food and beverages are available, and it's usually potluck (the guests bring something to share). A donation of $10 to $20 is collected at the door, which goes to support the touring musician. These days there are quite a number of folk musicians and singer/songwriters making a respectable living by traveling from house concert to house concert in towns and cities across the United States and Canada.

If you enjoy live music, consider hosting a series of house concerts—monthly, quarterly, or just try it once and see if you like it. If your living room is not large enough, you might want to partner with someone who has a more spacious home. Visit 2020CreativitySolution.com for information and references on how to put on a house concert. House concerts are an excellent way to get back to the intimate and active after-dinner creative experiences that were commonplace before the advent of radio and TV.

EXERCISE YOUR IMAGINATION

As I write this section I'm staring out the window of my mother-in-law's kitchen in upstate New York. There is a gentle veil of snow falling from the gray Northeastern sky as the winter birds flit around the trees and bird feeders. I'm reminded of my childhood, when I used to look out the window, daydreaming. Now I daydream consciously to exercise my imagination.

Daydream, my friends, daydream! Fantasize, let your

imagination run wild. Remember my elementary-school experiences of being reprimanded for daydreaming? The imagination is like a muscle. If you don't use it, it atrophies. I learned at an early age that I would get in trouble for using my imagination. So I stopped using it...at least in school. Eventually it faded in the rest of my life, too. If you begin using your imagination and exercising it from time to time, like a muscle, it becomes stronger. Brainstorm, free-write, or just look out the window and let your mind run free. I find that driving in the car really activates my imagination. Something about the way the scenery flies by gets my juices flowing. Imaginative qualities are not encouraged in our left-brain-dominant society, so we must make a conscious effort to develop them.

In *Imagination First*, Eric Liu and Scott Noppe-Brandon write: "Both innovation and creativity depend on imagination first: the ability and willingness to conceive of what is not. In times like these, imagination matters more than ever. And fortunately, it's something we all can cultivate—with practice."

Take a different route to work today. Go to a museum or visit some art galleries. Listen to jazz. Try using your nondominant hand more often. If you're right-handed, try using your left hand to do a free-write. See how that changes things. It'll take some practice, but it truly opens up new pathways of imagination in the brain. Singer/songwriter Susan Werner said this in her *Art of the Song* interview:

Here's something someone recommended to me once. I had a writer's block. She said, "Are you right-handed or are you left-handed?" I said, "I'm right-handed." She said, "Try writing in your notebook with your left hand. See what happens." Whatever your dominant hand is, take a notebook and pick up a pen and write with the opposite hand, and see what shows up. See what that handwriting looks like, and see what it says. Don't edit. Just let it show up. Every time I'm stuck, I'll do that.

I've gotten into the habit at meals—though I eat with my right hand—of drinking with my left hand. What about the great switch-hitters in baseball? I bet they're more balanced in their use of both hemispheres of the brain. Piano playing, guitar playing, the practice of most musical instruments develops dexterity in both hands.

My imagination began waking up when I started playing guitar in bands as a teenager. Learning to improvise guitar solos was difficult at first, but it was fun and I was motivated to learn. I studied the blues. While listening to great players like Eric Clapton, Mick Taylor, and Mike Bloomfield, I played along and learned their riffs and patterns on the fingerboard. Eventually I began coming up with original ideas and developing my own style.

HAVE FUN!

Fun is a key ingredient to living a creative lifestyle. Have fun with everything you do. You might ask, "How can I have fun at work or doing some chore that I don't like?" Fun is a choice. Every moment you can choose to have fun or not. Even the non-fun activities can be fun if you just shift your attitude a little. Of course you can choose to do more activities that you know are fun, and that fun will spill over into the rest of your life. Fun is an attitude. Fun is contagious. People will enjoy hanging out with you if you're fun to be around. You'll find yourself with more collabora-tive opportunities, and more creativity in all aspects of your life. Why not have fun? It's your choice.

KEY POINTS

1. Walk, shower, nap, visit nature—there are many things you can do to jump-start creativity.

2. Creativity begets creativity. That is, if you start doing little creative things in your life, creativity will naturally expand.

3. Creativity is all about having fun!

ACTION STEPS

1. Choose one of the tips suggested in this chapter, and make a plan to implement it in your life. For example, if you choose to take walks more often, you might write in your creativity journal, "I will go for an extended walk four days per week." Look at your calendar and block out the times you will walk this week.

2. Exercise your imagination. Reread the section on imagination and ask yourself how you can consciously exercise your imagination muscles. Write your thoughts in your creativity journal.

3. You're nearly finished with this book, and if you've done the action steps at the end of each chapter, and you've begun doing the 20-20 Practice, you've already increased the amount of creativity in your life. Now do a five-minute free-write in your creativity journal about how your newfound creativity has benefited you.

4. Circle or highlight the words and phrases that jump out at you in the free-write. Now write a short essay on the benefits of adding more creativity into your life. Send it to me at john@artofthesong.com.

7
Welcome to the Creative Renaissance

everyone has the **perfect gift** to give the
WORLD if each of us is freed up to give the
GIFT that is **uniquely** ours to give,
then the world will be in total **harmony**
—R. BUCKMINSTER FULLER,
philosopher and architect

CREATIVE RENAISSANCE

■ WHEN YOU INTEGRATE the three phases of creativity—inspiration, action, and analysis—into your life and apply them to your passion (that which you love to do), then you become unstoppable! In her *Art of the Song* interview, singer/songwriter Jonatha Brooke said, "Creativity is just a matter of what you're passionate about. It could be business, it could be law, it could be a doctor. Creativity is, I think, about passion." Passion is the power that drives the engine of creativity. Doing what you love gives you energy. Find what it is that you love doing. Study it. Practice it. Learn all you can about the subject. Excel at your passion and make your unique contribution to the world. When you integrate creativity into your life and apply yourself to your passion, you will accomplish great things and create a successful and happy life.

creativity is CENTRAL to any work that's worth doing, and creativity for me is one term for source or resourcefulness, SOURCE meaning going to the **essence of life**, going to the essence of spirit, actually OPENING yourself to be a channel for that which WANTS TO HAPPEN. creativity, I think, gives you a platform, or a place to stand, where you become the **generator of life** rather than a REACTOR to life, where you become the **creator** yourself of the world in which you want to live

—LYNNE TWIST
author of *The Soul of Money,*
interview for *Art of the Song*

As an added bonus of doing the 20-20 Practice, you just might find the doors to prosperity opening for you. Your Authentic Self is not only naturally creative but also naturally abundant. When you peel away the layers of ego and allow your creativity to flow, you open up your connection to the abundance of the universe. If you diligently do the work suggested in this book, you will gradually over time integrate with your Authentic Self. As you and your Authentic Self become one, you will begin to manifest infinite creativity and abundance in your life.

Can you imagine what the world would be like if everyone were just a little more creative—if we all added, say, ten percent more creativity into our lives? What if we used our rational minds for the wonderful tools that they are and put our intuitive minds back in the driver's seat? What if the arts were the *last* thing to be cut from school budgets? What if we actually *taught* creativity and the use of imagination in our schools?

I see that world. I see a renaissance in the arts, a flourishing of socially conscious businesses, a world where people are fulfilled and happy. I see a world where, through creativity, we have stopped global warming and developed alternative energy solutions: a world where we are no longer dependent on fossil fuels. I see a world where all people are contributing their own unique gifts and talents with passion and grace. I see a world that *works!*

As you have read, when we engage in a creative activity and lose ourselves in the creative flow, we access the spiritual part of ourselves and become connected with the Creator, God, the Holy Spirit, or whatever you choose to call it. If more and more people make this direct and real spiritual connection more often, things can't help but get better in our world.

Vivian and I have dedicated ourselves to this vision. Through radio, live presentations, seminars, individual coaching, and writing, we help people express their creativity. We remind them that they *are* creative at heart. Yes, some may have forgotten this basic truth, but with a little guidance and inspiration, anyone can access creativity. This is what we do; this is our mission.

Some people may be drawn to the arts, some may be inclined toward business or a helping profession, but whatever we do, if we do it with passion and creativity, we do our part in making the world a better place. It's about integrating right- and left-brain thinking, bringing the soul together with the mind, as my mentor Jim Folkman said. Its about bringing our whole consciousness to bear in whatever we do.

We're going through a major transition in our world at the time of this writing. Economic recession is forcing us to reexamine our priorities. Old ideas and forms are breaking down, slipping away. Businesses that operate on the old paradigm of greed and success at the expense of others are biting the dust. If you look at history, you'll see that many great civilizations were preceded by periods of darkness and despair. We are in one of those challenging times. Things may be difficult for many, but there has never been greater opportunity, greater hope. Through creativity we can turn that hope into reality.

Creativity is contagious, just like laughter. The benefits are real. I invite you to use the 20-20 Practice to focus your natural creativity, and as you do, please join us in spreading the creative message. Help us all move into the Creative Renaissance!

LOVE AND FEAR

When I was in my early twenties I spent two years traveling back and forth across the country and up and down the West Coast, living on the road. I had no money. All I owned was a guitar, a sleeping bag, and the pack on my back. You could say I was a professional traveler. Hitchhiking was my primary mode of transportation, and I'd share songs and stories in exchange for rides and food. I befriended a guy named Charlie who showed me the ropes and even taught me how to catch a ride on a freight train.[1] I traveled with Charlie for several months, learning all I could, before eventually going solo.

---

1. Disclaimer: Riding freight trains is illegal and very dangerous. Do not attempt to ride on a freight train. You could be seriously injured or die!

Creativity was at the very heart of our existence on the road. Our survival depended upon it. One of Charlie's tricks was to bet that he could feed everyone in the car for less than five dollars, and he guaranteed that it would be something they'd never eaten before *and* it would be good. All they had to do was put up the five dollars. Charlie would then buy a dozen eggs, a loaf of bread, some butter, and a head of cabbage, and he would make this surprisingly delicious "cabbage omelet." Here's a song I wrote about those times, "Travelin' with Charlie":

Charlie wore a little brass bell that would tinkle as he'd walk
He'd tell you 'bout his endless trip, he couldn't help but talk
His hair was like a lion's mane and the sun had parched his skin
You could see the gap between his teeth 'cause he always had a grin

He taught me how to get along on the road without a dime
We'd hitch a ride to who knows where, tell stories, and share good times
We'd keep a list of friends we'd made in towns from coast to coast
We'd always find a place to stay, eat cabbage, eggs, and toast

Travelin' with Charlie, travelin' free
Like the Santa Ana winds we'd blow
From the mountains to the sea
Travelin' with Charlie, travelin' free
It must have been the Lord above
Was watchin' over Charlie and me

He showed me how to ride the rails into the morning light
We'd head on down to the railroad yard in the middle of the night
We'd ask the late-shift workers which train was goin' where
We'd find an empty boxcar and by morning we'd be out of there

Travelin' with Charlie, travelin' free
Like the Santa Ana winds we'd blow
From the mountains to the sea
Travelin' with Charlie, travelin' free
It must have been the Lord above
Was watchin' over Charlie and me

Each day we blaze a brand-new trail by foot, by thumb, or rail
From time to time we'd cross the line and spend a night in jail

He was a vagrant in the eyes of the law, some called him a bum
But Charlie was my travelin' guide, he taught me how to thumb
He shared the beauty of the land and he lived by this creed:
"You'll never wind up down and out if you make friends and
*   do good deeds"*

Travelin' with Charlie, travelin' free
Like the Santa Ana winds we'd blow
From the mountains to the sea
Travelin' with Charlie, travelin' free
It must have been the Lord above
Was watchin' over Charlie and me

There is a free audio download of "Travelin' with Charlie" at 2020CreativitySolution.com.

Being out there on the road was a lonely place, with lots of time to think about the meaning of life and such. It was very scary at times. Sometimes fear would creep into my mind and totally take over. "What if I get picked up by a bunch of rednecks and they beat the shit out of me? What if the cops pick me up and put me in jail?" (Which actually happened a few times.) And then there were times when I truly felt alive with a strong sense of freedom and self-confidence, with love and compassion for my fellow human beings. In those times, amazing and synchronistic events occurred often. It felt like I was being "cared for" by a higher power. These were the times when I was aligned with my Authentic Self.

The interesting thing was that even though I had no money, all my needs were always met. Almost every day I'd have a good meal or two and a roof to sleep under. I was happy and successful...penniless yet prosperous! I truly experienced the natural abundance of the universe. I remember one time I had gotten a ride in Oregon and was dropped off in the middle of Eugene. It was near the university campus, and I was feeling particularly happy and grateful. No sooner had I jumped out of the car than a man, who looked like a college professor, came up to me and handed me a five-dollar bill (you could buy a lot with $5 in those days). He said, "You look like you could use this."

I remember another amazing thing that happened the time Charlie and I were getting off a train in Cheyenne, Wyoming. Well, no sooner had the train pulled to a stop than a van full of friendly folks pulled up next to our boxcar and said, "Get in! Come with us." They gave us a hot meal and a warm place to stay for the night, and drove us out to the freeway the next morning.

One time, I turned what would appear to be a very negative experience into a positive one. I was picked up for hitchhiking on Interstate 80 in Akron, Ohio. Because I had no money to pay the fine, I was arrested and locked up in the county jail for three days. I happened to have a book (given to me the day before by my friend Wanda in Cincinnati) on the subject of meditation, astral travel, and other mystical things. Not wanting to dwell on my physical surroundings, I used the time in jail to read and practice meditating. I was able to connect with my Authentic Self through meditation and literally transcend the walls of the prison. I knew at a very deep level the truth of what Pierre Teilhard de Chardin said centuries ago—that I was an infinite spiritual being having a human experience. The three days in jail flew by like three hours!

The other night I went to sleep with the tune and lyrics to "Travelin' with Charlie" going through my head. Later that night I found myself in a dream reliving and re-creating the events—some real and some imagined—of those years. In the dream I was explaining my life to someone. I woke up in the middle of the night and wrote some notes down. This is what came in my writing the next morning:

> In those years I liked to tell people that my whole life was "at the mercy of the wind." I totally put myself out there, at risk, and I simply surrendered to whatever the universe had in store for me. At the time it was easy to see that my life was a continuous chain of events happening one after another, and that they were all interrelated and interconnected. My life was a series of rides from one place to the next punctuated by periods of standing or walking down the highway waiting for the next ride. It's like this, you realize that if one thing—one link in the chain—hadn't happened, then the thing that happened the next ride or two rides later wouldn't have happened either. If you hadn't been standing out in the rain three days ago, you never would have wound up where you are now. So you learn to be grateful for the good times and the bad 'cause they're all part of some higher plan. But you also learn that the happier you are, the more good times you'll have, and the good will outweigh the bad.

When you put yourself out there "at the mercy of the wind" like I did, you open yourself up to the synchronistic flow of the universe. You have no choice but to live in the present moment. In twelve-step recovery programs there is a step where we turn our will and our lives over to the care of a higher power. Though I didn't know it at the time, this is what I was doing. By the way, you don't have to give away all your money and go hitchhiking to apply these principles in your life!

During those years I learned several life lessons, but the most valuable was the distinction between love and fear, and how those forces played out in my life. When I was feeling good and putting out good energy (love), good things would happen. I wouldn't have to wait long for rides, and I would get picked up by interesting and friendly people. But when I allowed fear to creep in, I would find myself standing in the same place for hours and hours, sometimes overnight, before getting a ride. I learned that we have a choice every moment. We can live out of love, or we can live out of fear. Love makes us magnetic to good people and circumstances, and fear repels them. The more often we choose love, the better our lives become. Some call it karma, some call it the golden rule, but I learned in my traveling years that there was tremendous value in staying positive and treating people with love and respect. I believe we are all naturally good, and that creative expression gives us an opportunity to tap into that naturally good and creative part of ourselves. I invite you to choose love and creativity for a life full of happiness and success.

Are you the college professor who gave me the five-dollar bill in Eugene, Oregon? Maybe you're one of the hundreds of people kind enough to give me a ride during those traveling years. Do you play a Dillon Guitar? Did we meet in the floral business? Perhaps you're a devoted *Art of the Song* listener, or maybe this book is our first encounter. However it is that we are connected, I extend my sincere gratitude to you, and I encourage you to share your unique gift with the world. I invite you to paint that beautiful work of art on the canvas that is your life. Write that symphony with notes that are the minutes and hours of your every day.

I am a DIVINE CREATIVE being full of **passion** and **grace**
my every act is one of **creation**
I MANIFEST in the world word by word, note by note
my world is a SYMPHONY of **creativity**

ACTION STEPS

Congratulations! You've finished reading *The 20-20 Creativity Solution*, and if you've begun doing the practice and applying the principles in the book, it's likely you're seeing some positive changes in your life.

1. JOIN THE RENAISSANCE

As more and more people integrate with their Authentic Selves and express their creativity, there is a subtle shift in the energy of the planet. If you believe, like I do, that we are on the verge of a great creative renaissance, then you understand how important it is to encourage one another to do this work. Let's team up to spread the creative message. If you have any friends or acquaintances who might benefit from reading this book, please invite them to order a copy at the2020book.com. Or, as many others have done, purchase several copies yourself and give them as gifts. Together we can make a difference.

2. BE THE CHANGE

I want to make it easy for you to integrate the 20-20 Practice into your life, so I've put together a special program to help you get started with my guidance, and with the support and accountability of a group. I call it the 20-20 JumpStart. There are many benefits of doing the practice with a group: inspiration, discussion, camaraderie, tapping into the group creative energy, and just knowing there are others out there doing the practice. So, I strongly encourage you to go to 2020JumpStart.com and sign up for the next JumpStart group that will be forming soon.

And remember, there are many other
resources and free gifts available at:

2020CreativitySolution.com

Hope to see you there!

Recommended Reading and Resources

Patricia Aburdene, *Megatrends 2010* (Charlottesville, VA: Hampton Roads, 2005)

Jamie Andreas, Guitar Principles, available at guitarprinciples.com

ArtoftheSong.org/stations for a list and map of stations carrying *Art of the Song: Creativity Radio*

Julia Cameron, *The Artist's Way* (New York: Tarcher/ Putnam, 1992)

Jack Canfield with Janet Switzer, *The Success Principles* (New York: William Morrow, 2004)

Deepak Chopra, e-mail newsletter, November 2009, available at chopra.com/agni/nov09

Deepak Chopra, *The Ultimate Happiness Prescription* (New York: Harmony, 2009)

Mihaly Csikszentmihalyi, *Creativity* (New York: Harper Collins, 1996)

Judy Collins, *Morning, Noon and Night* (New York: Penguin Group, 2005)

Dianne Crampton, *TIGERS Among Us* (Bend, OR: Three Creeks Publishing, 2010)

Dr. Wayne Dyer, *The Power of Intention* (Carlsbad, CA: Hay House, Inc., 2004)

Suzanne Falter-Barns, *Eight Quick Ways to Nurture Creativity*, available at hinduwebsite.com getknownnow.com

Richard Florida, *The Rise of the Creative Class* (New York: Basic Books, 2002)

Matthew Fox, *Creativity: Where the Divine and the Human Meet* (New York: Tarcher/Penguin, 2002)

Terry Garthwaite, founding member of the 1960s San Francisco Bay Area group "Joy of Cooking," terrygarthwaite.com

David Cameron Gikandi, *A Happy Pocket Full of Money* (Bloomington, IN: Xlibris Corporation, 2008)

Thich Nhat Hanh, *Living Buddha, Living Christ* (New York: Penguin, 1995, 2007)

Allegra Huston, *Love Child: A Memoir of Family Lost and Found* (New York: Simon & Schuster, 2009); allegrahuston.com

Eric Liu and Scott Noppe-Brandon, *Imagination First: Unlocking the Power of Possibility* (Hoboken, NJ: John Wiley & Sons, 2009)

John Daido Loori, *The Zen of Creativity: Cultivating Your Artistic Life* (New York: Ballantine Books, 2004)

Eric Maisel, *Sleep Thinking*, download available at 2020CreativitySolution.com

Eric Maisel, *Ten Zen Seconds* (Naperville, IL: Sourcebooks, 2007)

Eric Maisel, John Dillon, and Vivian Nesbitt, TeleSummits.com

The Painting Experience, processarts.com

Daniel Pink, *A Whole New Mind* (New York: Penguin, 2005)

Paul Ray and Sherry Anderson, *The Cultural Creatives* (New York: Harmony Books, 2002); culturalcreatives.org

Herman Rednick, *The Earth Journey* (New York: Vantage Press, 1980)

Paul Reisler, Kid Pan Alley, kidpanalley.org

Sir Ken Robinson, *The Element* (New York: Penguin, 2009)

Rumi, *The Essential Rumi*, Coleman Barks et al., translators (San Francisco: Harper San Francisco, 1995)

Thomas Ryan, *Soul Fire: Accessing your Creativity* (Woodstock, VT: SkyLight Paths Publishing, 2008)

Jamie Sams, *Dancing the Dream* (New York: HarperCollins, 1999)

Therese Schmid, *Promoting Health Through Creativity* (New York: John Wiley & Sons, 2005)

Roger W. Sperry and Eran Zaidel, *Lateral Specialization of Cerebral Function in the Surgically Separated Hemispheres*, 14th Annual Meeting of the Psychonomic Society, 1973

Jill Bolte Taylor, *My Stroke of Insight* (New York: Penguin, 2009)

Michael Toms, *The Well of Creativity* (Carlsbad, CA: Hay House, 1997)

Lynne Twist, *The Soul of Money* (New York: Norton, 2006)

Brenda Ueland, *If You Want to Write* (New York: Putnam, 1938)

Art of the Song
Contributing Guests

Our gratitude goes out to the following *Art of the Song* guests whose interviews were excerpted or ideas were referenced for this book:

Jonatha Brooke
Beth Nielsen Chapman
Guy Clark
Bruce Cockburn
Mary Gauthier
Dave Gibson
Sara Hickman
Meg Hutchinson
James Navé
Paul Reisler
Karen Savoca
Lynne Twist
Susan Werner